In the Footsteps of a Saint

John Paul II's Visit to Wisconsin

Philip Kosloski

WESTBOW
PRESS

A DIVISION OF THOMAS NELSON
& ZONDERVAN

WestBow Press books may be ordered through booksellers or by contacting:

WestBow Press
A Division of Thomas Nelson & Zondervan
1663 Liberty Drive
Bloomington, IN 47403
www.westbowpress.com
1 (866) 928-1240

ISBN: 978-1-4908-7204-9 (sc)
ISBN: 978-1-4908-7206-3 (hc)
ISBN: 978-1-4908-7205-6 (e)

Library of Congress Control Number: 2015903531

Print information available on the last page.

WestBow Press rev. date: 03/10/2015

Contents

Pronunciation Guide

Częstochowa = *Chens-toe-HOE-vah*

Dziwisz = *JEE*-vish

Kraków = *KRA-koov*

Potocki = *Po-TUTS-ki*

Stanisław = *Stah-NEES-wahv*

Waclaw = *VAH-clav*

Wojtyła = *Voy-TEE-wah*

Wujek = *VOO-yek*

Wyszynski = *Vih-SHIN-skee*

Introduction

The JPII Generation

It was April 2, 2005. I was a senior in high school when I heard the pope had died. The fact of his death did not surprise me, as everyone knew his health had been declining rapidly over the past few months, yet I was still saddened by the news. Growing up Catholic, I knew John Paul II was our pope and, at the same time, he was the only pope I ever knew. I was not alone as my generation of Catholics would become known as the "JPII Generation." I did not know him very well as I had only just begun to investigate the Catholic faith into which I had been born. However, even though my knowledge and familiarity with John Paul II was minimal, I knew one thing—he was Polish.

While it appears to be a trivial piece of information, for a young high school student growing up in a rural Polish community, it gave me a connection whereby I felt like he was a part of my own family. My ancestors came from the same country and so, in a way, we shared the same "Polish blood." It may seem unlikely that a high school student would feel such a strong connection to an elderly and fragile pope living half-way across the world, but when you live in a community that is proud of its Polish heritage it is easy to become proud of anyone who is Polish and instantly feel that he is family. This strong familial bond even led me to make a memorial to the great Polish pope on the outside of my high school locker. The memorial quickly grew from a few pictures and a quote, to include a rose left anonymously by a fellow student. Before I had done this, the public high school I attended had instituted a ban on posting anything on the outside of one's locker. The lockers were new and the administration did not want them to wear too quickly. Thankfully, after looking at my locker the school officials decided that I had not defaced the lockers and allowed me to keep the memorial. For them, honoring the life of a Catholic pope did not fall into the category of "trouble-making."

After paying my own tribute to the Polish pope, I heard of a memorial Mass being offered at Saint Peter Catholic Church in Stevens Point in honor of John Paul II. This was close to my hometown and easy enough to attend, so I drove to the evening Mass to offer my own prayers for his soul. Upon arrival, I was greeted by a slew of tables set up in the entryway. On them were pictures and news articles about the visit of a "Cardinal Wojtyła" to Stevens Point. In fact, this same cardinal had even made a visit to the church in which I was standing. I soon found out that Cardinal Wojtyła visited the area two years prior to being elected Pope John Paul II. I was stunned to find out this information and immediately felt a closer connection to the deceased pontiff. Not only did he share my "blood," but he walked in the very same places that I walked! The memorial Mass was packed with Poles and others from the Stevens Point area and left me with an amazing feeling of closeness to the man who inspired the whole world.

A Saint before he was a Saint

As I began to research the two short days he was in central Wisconsin, I quickly realized that John Paul II left a lasting impact upon the people. Everyone was drawn to him, which is strange since he was an unknown Polish cardinal who visited a small rural community in the middle of nowhere. It is interesting that even before Wojtyła set foot on Wisconsin soil, the organizers had a sense that his visit would attract thousands of people. The initial estimate was that over 10,000 people would attend an open air Mass celebrated by the Polish cardinal! In my research I found both non-Catholics and non-believers attracted to him. It became evident to me that this book would become much more than a mere compilation of stories of days gone by, but a testament to John Paul II's lifelong saintly character. His little visit to Wisconsin clearly shows that he began inspiring people with his holy life long before he took center stage in the world as Pope John Paul II and his magnetic personality was just beginning to gain a following that would later result in millions of people clamoring to see even just a glimpse of him at a distance.

Walking in his footsteps

In researching this book, I have spent hours upon hours leafing through old newspapers at the Archives in the library of the University of Wisconsin-Stevens Point as well as meeting various people who were present at Cardinal Wojtyła's visit. While I was doing this, I felt as if I was walking in his footsteps, tracing the steps he took and discovering the many lives that he touched. Saints have a tendency to do that. Wherever they go, they inspire the people and places they meet for decades, centuries (even millennia) afterwards.

For example, millions of pilgrims flock every year to Saint Peter's basilica in Rome to see the final resting place of a simple fisherman who became the first pope of the Catholic Church. At the same time, not only do pilgrims pay their respects to the place where Saint Peter is buried, they also visit a church in Rome where the chains are currently housed that bound Saint Peter when he was imprisoned in Jerusalem.

In the Catholic tradition, anything that touches the body of a canonized saint is called a relic. These items, which can be anything from gloves they wore to chalices a saint used while celebrating Mass, are treasured in the same way a widow treasures the tools her husband used everyday of his life. Relics of a saint are a special remembrance of a person who lived a life of sanctity and brings us close to them here on earth. It helps us realize that this man or woman of extraordinary holiness was a real person and not just a myth or fairy tale. They walked upon this earth just like us and we can now ask for their intercession as they gaze upon the face of God in Heaven.

What I hope for this book is to preserve the memory and "relics" of John Paul II's visit to Wisconsin. This saint who literally changed the world, visited an obscure part of the country and spoke to simple Polish farmers as if he were a long lost relative. The ground he walked and the places he visited are now true relics, places where we can go to follow in his footsteps and praise God that he gave us such a worthy man to emulate. John Paul II's example of simplicity, humility and holiness that he gave to the Polish people of central Wisconsin on those two short days in 1976 is not only meant to inspire those who live close by. His witness of faith should encourage anyone on the journey of life and show that being a saint doesn't mean being divorced from this world, but actually entails being a part of it. In these pages, I pray that you will see a simple man who remained very human on his own path to sanctity.

- Philip Kosloski

PART I

The Early Life of Karol Wojtyła

CHAPTER I

Lolek

In 1975, the United States media outlets were abuzz with the announcement that the next International Eucharistic Congress would be held in the City of Brotherly Love: Philadelphia. It had been almost fifty years since the congress was held in North America, and three years prior, it had been held in Melbourne, Australia. Ever since the inception of the Eucharistic Congress at the end of the nineteenth century, thousands upon thousands of pilgrims from almost every country would travel many miles to attend these important gatherings. The goal of the congress was to unite Catholics from around the world in an event that would strengthen their personal faith and reinvigorate their belief in the Real Presence of Jesus Christ in the Eucharist (hence the name, Eucharistic Congress). This is one of the most important doctrines in the Catholic Church.

When Dr. Waclaw Soroka, professor of Russian and East European history at the University of Wisconsin-Stevens Point, heard it was going to be in the United States, he immediately sought to discover who would attend from his native Poland. At first, he wasn't sure who would come, but it was understood that a large delegation of Polish priests and bishops would travel to Philadelphia. Not only would these Poles be present for the conferences in Philadelphia, but it was made clear that they desired to travel to various communities of Polish descent. Dr. Soroka knew what he had to do: he needed to invite Cardinal Stefan Wyszynski to Wisconsin.

At the time, Cardinal Wyszynski was the Primate of Poland, which meant he was entrusted with a unique leadership over all Catholics in that country. His influence extended over both the clergy and laity in Poland, and he acted as a vocal spokesman for the Church. Because of his visibly important position, Cardinal Wyszynski was under fire when the communists took control of the government. Yet throughout the years of the Cold War, Cardinal Wyszynski stood firm amid intense pressure from those in power, not allowing Catholicism to be stamped out.

On account of Cardinal Wyszynski's position, as well as his unwavering resistance to communism, Dr. Soroka sought to invite him to central Wisconsin to give a talk at a newly established organization called the Annual Lectures on Poland. Dr. Soroka knew "Father" Wyszynski well, as both had been active at the University of Lublin during the Nazi occupation. Dr. Soroka wanted to ensure that Cardinal Wyszynski accepted the invitation, so he passed it through Wyszynski's close friend Dr. Konstanty Turowski. Unfortunately, the Primate was not attending the congress in Philadelphia and could not accept the invitation. Cardinal Wyszynski had another idea: invite a close colleague of his, whom he called the "other Polish cardinal."

At the time, Poland had only two cardinals. Cardinal Wyszynski was referring to Cardinal Karol Wojtyła, the young archbishop of Krakow. He would be leading the delegation of bishops to Philadelphia and was most likely to accept the invitation. While Cardinal Wojtyła was not his first choice, Dr. Soroka decided to ask him to be the keynote speaker at the event in central Wisconsin.[1]

············----------············

Who Is Karol Wojtyła?

Karol Józef Wojtyła was born on May 18, 1920, in Wadowice, Poland, to Karol and Emilia Wojtyła. The youngest of three children, Karol had an older brother named Edmund and a sister who died in infancy. At the time of his birth, Karol's father was a noncommissioned officer who would later retire on pension around 1927.[2] Karol's mother, Emilia, stayed at home with her children in their small, but comfortable apartment. She helped support the family by using her expertise in embroidery as an extra source of income.[3] When she wasn't sewing, she was sitting with neighbors as her little Karol, whom she affectionately called Lolek, played in the courtyard.[4]

The Wojtyła family lived in a simple, middle-class apartment across from St. Mary's Church in Wadowice.[5] Karol's loving parents strove to raise their children to be faithful Catholics in the great tradition of their ancestors. Poland was (and still is) a nation inhabited by an overwhelming majority of Catholics. It seemed everyone was Catholic, which led to a strong Catholic culture where the faith was simply a part of daily life. Yet Karol would have to endure great suffering even in his early life to persevere in the faith of his ancestors.

Nine years after Karol's birth, his mother died from kidney failure and heart disease.[6] Three short years later, in 1932, Karol's brother Edmund also died, leaving Karol and his father the only remaining members of the Wojtyła family.[7] This second blow hit Karol hard, as his brother Edmund was his childhood playmate who had taught him how to ski and often played soccer with him in the streets of Wadowice.[8]

Karol's death-filled childhood was not easy, but two things were certain: Karol and his father would draw closer together through their suffering, and the two would learn to support each other in an ever-changing Poland.

The Wojtyła Seminary

Karol, now in the midst of his education at a local high school, would learn from his father how to be a man. Drawing from his own time in the military, Karol's father developed a rigorous schedule that they both kept each day. Rising early in the morning, father and son would say their morning prayers, attend the morning Mass at seven o'clock, and eat breakfast before school started.[9] Karol became a faithful altar boy and served the daily Mass he attended with his father. At the end of the school day, there was time for play, homework, and walks together after supper. They would read the Bible together, pray the rosary, and discuss how the life of faith was more about deep, interior conversion than empty, exterior acts.

Looking back at the childhood days with his father, John Paul II reflected upon his eternal gratitude for the example of his father, who provided for him his "first seminary" and gave him the foundation needed to continue in his quest for holiness.[10] It would also provide the first seeds of a vocation to the priesthood, although at the beginning, he was reluctant to accept the call of the Lord.

Looking ahead to his future, young Karol was engrossed with the idea of studying literature and drama and becoming an actor. In high school, he participated in many theatrical productions and was captivated by the rich literary tradition of Poland. As a result, he committed himself to attend the historic Jagiellonian University, where he would become immersed in Polish literature. Realizing his son's potential, Karol Sr. moved with his son to Kraków and found an apartment that the two would share. Once enrolled in the Jagiellonian, he participated with his college friends in local plays and poetry readings, while studying the depths of language. Everything was going smoothly after his first year of university, and Karol was on track to become a great actor.

This would all change in 1939.

Adolf Hitler, in a move to expand and reclaim lands that had once been a part of the German Empire before World War I, as well as to replenish supplies for his ongoing war, mobilized his army and invaded Poland on September 1, 1939. At the same time, Russia also began its invasion of Poland from the east. Poland was hemmed in on all fronts. There was no escape.

Karol Wojtyła and his father, after an unsuccessful attempt to flee to the east, returned to Kraków to find the Nazi flag everywhere. They retreated to their apartment and were now subject to one of the most terrible regimes in history. It did not take long for the Nazis to make their presence felt as they quickly enacted a full-scale campaign to wipe out any memory of Poland or its culture. On November 9, 184 professors of the Jagiellonian University were shipped off to a concentration camp where most would lose their lives. The Nazis knew that in order to have absolute control over a nation, they needed to sever that nation from its cultural and intellectual pursuits. They needed to control every aspect of citizens' lives, especially their minds, to ensure that there would never be a revolt.

With the dissolution of the Jagiellonian University, Karol was now forced to secure a work card or risk being shipped off to a concentration camp. Polish citizens needed to be "useful," and anyone who did not perform a specific function was either arrested or killed on sight. Still in the prime of his youth and deemed useful to Nazi society, Karol secured a job at a nearby rock quarry. Karol spent a full year in the harsh conditions of the quarry as a manual laborer, and the strenuous job became the only source of income for Karol and his father. Yet it was in this quarry that Karol would reflect upon the great dignity of human work, and his time there later influenced his own writings on the topic. At the same time, although much of his days were spent at the quarry, he also participated in an underground movement to ensure the survival of Polish culture.

The Rhapsodic Theatre

The Nazis' attempt to stamp out any remnant of Polish culture proved to have the opposite effect. Soon after the Nazi invasion, Karol conspired with his literary colleagues to have a poetry reading at a friend's house. Karol and his group of friends knew that in order to keep Poland alive, they needed to preserve the arts. In particular, they focused on preserving Poland through the riches of its native language. This small group not only recited poetry but also performed classic Polish plays under the cover of night in the apartments of faithful supporters. Over the years, Poland had suffered much in the way of foreign control of its land, yet it was always culture and faith in God that kept Poland united.

This underground group of actors would be known as the "Rhapsodic Theatre," or in other words, "The Theatre of the Word." Wojtyła co-founded this group along with his mentor, Dr. Mieczysław Kotlarczyk, who helped shape the vision of the small troupe. Dr. Kotlarczyk was a devout Christian actor in Kraków and he devoted his entire life to the theatre. Wojtyła was drawn to him because of his new theatrical vision, which was unheard of at the time. Kotlarczyk's new type of drama sought to "explore the depths of the human soul rather than focus on the external events of conventional drama."[11] They accomplished this goal while performing powerful dramas, especially the classics of Polish Romanticism. What set their productions apart was a type of theatre that relied heavily on the vocal performance of the actors and had very minimal use of sets, costumes and props. Karol thrived as an actor in the "Rhapsodic Theatre" and hoped he could continue to perform for years to come.

Yet, Karol's life would change dramatically with the passing of his father. Affectionately known as "the Captain," Karol the elder died on February 18, 1941. The young Karol Wojtyła was now an orphan at age twenty. The loss of his father affected Karol deeply. Before his father's burial, Karol spent many nights in prayer at the side of his father's body.

His father's death marked a new chapter in Karol's life. It forced him to think not only about his father and the impact he had, but also about which direction he was headed. Karol began to scrutinize his own decisions more closely and the path before him became clearer and clearer. The event of his father's death jolted his conscience and he felt he could no longer put off what was in the back of his mind. He knew that he might be called to the priesthood and started to detach himself from the theater and his career as an actor. This was not easy, as many of his theatre friends begged him to stay and develop his God-given talents. Karol, however, could not be dissuaded. He felt the first urgings to priestly service when he was a child, but now the calling only began to increase and he could no longer deny it. A year and a half later in 1942, Karol made the first step by knocking on the door of Franciszkanska, 3, the residence of Archbishop Adam Stefan Sapieha, and boldly proclaimed: "I want to become a priest."[12]

CHAPTER II

The Other Polish Cardinal

Under Nazi occupation the Catholic Church in Poland was under tight surveillance. Religion was an area of life that the Nazis wanted to dominate and, as a result, the Gestapo put heavy restrictions on training new priests. Because of these restrictions, Archbishop Sapieha was forced to move his seminary completely underground. This action was due in large part to the arrest of five seminary students who were sent to Auschwitz, never to be seen again.

The young Karol Wojtyła realized the risk he was taking yet still felt called to serve the people of God as an ordained priest. Karol studied hard during the night shift he was given at a local chemical factory. This was a risk, as he could have easily been reported to his supervisors for neglecting his duties. Providentially Karol's fellow workers did not bother him, allowing him to continue his clandestine studies. It was not easy for Karol to live a double life, and it remained extremely dangerous. One morning at the Archbishop's residence, a fellow seminarian and friend of Wojtyła never arrived to serve Mass. The Gestapo had arrested him during the night, and Karol later found out that his friend was scheduled to be executed. It was only by God's divine hand that Karol would survive the war and become a priest.

The German occupation of Kraków ended on January 18, 1945, and those in the city began to rebuild all that was lost during the war. The citizens would not rejoice for long. Russia quickly moved in to take control of Poland and sought to reign with its own oppressive Communist agenda. Poland was still not free.

The Soviets quickly filled the void the Nazis had left. The swastika was replaced by the hammer and sickle; the totalitarian dictatorship was traded for the reign of atheistic communism. While it did not prove to be an ideal situation, the Polish people were granted more freedom than they had experienced under the Nazis. Intellectual life was allowed to reemerge, which resulted in the resurrection of the historic Jagiellonian University. Karol Wojtyla was able to complete his theological studies and finish preparations for the priesthood.

Father Karol Wojtyła

After passing examinations and a rigorous month of spiritual exercises, Karol Jozef Wojtyła was ordained to the holy priesthood on All Saints' Day, 1946, in the private chapel of Cardinal Sapieha. While Karol was ordained a priest on one of the most joyous days in the liturgical year, his first day as a priest occurred on one of the most somber—All Souls' Day. On November 2, Father Wojtyła celebrated three Masses and offered them for his mother, brother, and father, respectively. It was a day of joy and sorrow; Karol rejoiced in the glory of the priesthood but also mourned that his parents and brother could not be present with him. He knew that offering the Mass for the repose of their souls was the greatest gift a priest could offer.

A few weeks after being ordained, Father Wojtyła was ordered to complete his doctoral studies. He packed up his few belongings and boarded a train to Rome. It was the first time he had ever left the borders of his native homeland. Karol made himself at home in the Eternal City and remained there for two years, studying at the Pontifical University of Saint Thomas Aquinas (Angelicum) in order to achieve a doctorate in Theology. While Father Wojtyła enjoyed his time in Rome, he was much more eager to complete his studies and return to the Fatherland to begin ministry as a priest. At last, in the summer of 1948, Father Wojtyła returned to Poland and was assigned to be a vicar at a country parish.

Nestled in the foothills of the Carpathian Mountains outside of Kraków, Father Wojtyła's first assignment proved to set the stage for the kind of priest he would be. Arriving at his new assignment he got off the bus, walked for several miles and took a shortcut that went through the fields of grain. Father Wojtyla reached the small parish church and felt inspired to kneel and kiss the dirty ground. The action showed the people that he had a great respect for them and their traditions and further revealed his desire to be one with them in the joys and trials of life. Father Wojtyła put much effort into being present among his people. He often trudged through the winter snow in his worn, dirty cassock and made individual visits to each house in the parish. This was a mighty task as the country parish served fourteen nearby villages and included five elementary schools.[13] As a result of this humble, personalized style of leadership, the parishioners loved their young and zealous priest and grew very close to him. They respected his simplicity and the genuine care he showed them.

"Uncle"

He did not stay long at this peaceful and idyllic location in the countryside. After a mere eight months working in the parish, Karol was taken out of parish ministry and moved back to the city. Father Wojtyła was assigned as the chaplain for the Jagiellonian University and was stationed at St. Florian's Church in Kraków. It was there that Father Wojtyła flourished as a priest and attracted the attention of the young university students.

The students were instantly drawn to this intellectually gifted priest, who was not a snobby professor but a simple and energetic man. He started up numerous initiatives to reinvigorate Polish culture, giving frequent lectures and forming a group of young adults who even read their way through the entire *Summa Theologiae*—in Latin. It was not only his zealous actions that attracted many young people, but also his numerous excursions into the wilderness. He led groups of students on weeklong hikes and ski trips. Father Wojtyła was an avid outdoorsman and loved being surrounded by the natural beauty of creation. He also participated in many athletic events, including an international kayaking competition. Quickly a close-knit group of young people formed around this dynamic and adventurous priest, which resulted in many life-long friendships. To them he was no longer "Father Wojtyła," but *"Wujek"* ("Uncle").[14]

St. Florian's Church grew year after year and Father Wojtyła's unique ability to connect with university students was clearly seen by all. As a result, he was given two years to attain the credentials of a university professor and then was quickly appointed to the philosophy department at the University of Lublin. During this time Father Wojtyła remained in contact with his group of friends in Kraków and continued to go on excursions in the country. As a priest and professor, Father Wojtyła attracted young people wherever he went, but he also possessed a great mind and battled with many of the leading intellectuals at the university. He was a man everyone felt at ease with, and his magnanimity did not go unnoticed.

Father Wojtyła remained at the University of Lubin until 1958, when at the age of thirty-eight he was appointed an auxiliary bishop of the Archdioccse of Kraków and became the youngest bishop in Poland. Wojtyła received word of his new assignment while kayaking with friends.

Father Karol Wojtyła was ordained a bishop on September 28, 1958, at Wawel Cathedral in Kraków. He took for his episcopal motto the phrase *"Totus Tuus."* The phrase is a shortened version of a prayer by St. Louis de Montfort regarding consecration to the Blessed Virgin Mary. The full phrase in Latin reads: *Totus tuus ego sum, et omnia mea tua sunt. Accipio te in mea omnia. Praebe mihi cor tuum, Maria* (I belong entirely to you, and all that I have is yours. I take you for my all. O Mary, give me your heart.). Bishop Wojtyła firmly believed that the closer a person drew towards Mary, the closer he came to Christ. He would keep this motto and live by it for the rest of his life.

As an auxiliary bishop, Karol was introduced into a whole new world of activity. He was asked to travel throughout the archdiocese of Kraków to minister to the numerous spiritual needs of the faithful. At the same time, he remained close to his friends at the Jagiellonian University and continued to preach and give retreats for students. He even maintained his yearly tradition of venturing out into the wilderness to kayak and ski with his close-knit group of friends. Even though he was now a bishop, he remained *Wujek* and did not allow his new hierarchal position to prevent him from being the joyful and adventurous man that his friends knew him to be.

The Council That Would Change the World

After a few short years of experience as a shepherd for the Archdiocese of Kraków, Bishop Wojtyła was asked to participate in what became one of the most monumental events of the twentieth century in the Catholic Church: the Second Vatican Council. Between the years of 1962 and 1965, Wojtyła traveled to Rome and participated in numerous sessions during which the future of the Church in the modern world was intensely discussed.

Throughout the numerous debates, Bishop Wojtyła informed his flock in Poland about the primary "spirit" of the Council. He made frequent broadcasts on Vatican Radio to the Polish people and focused on the "spiritual renewal" that was intended to be the main theme of Vatican II. He combated any desire of the Polish media to portray the different factions of the Council. Instead he stressed the beautiful fruit that arose from discussions on the dignity of the human person and the role of the laity in the modern world. He wanted to ensure that the people of his Archdiocese were not misled by the erroneous political agendas often broadcasted by the Western media.

Among the plethora of sessions and debates in which Bishop Wojtyła participated, his presence was most felt in the formation of the document on the *Pastoral Constitution on the Church in the Modern World* (*Gaudium et Spes*), as well as the *Dogmatic Constitution on the Church* (*Lumen Gentium*). In these two documents Wojtyła brought to the Council not only his years of philosophical studies, but more importantly his experience working with the common man: understanding his needs, wants, and desires. His presence and expertise were certainly felt at the Council and did not go unnoticed by the hierarchy of the Church.

A Successor to Saint Stanisław

Several years before the conclusion of the Second Vatican Council, Archbishop Eugeniusz Baziak of Kraków died and his See was left vacant for over eighteen months. The delay in the appointment and installation of his successor was due in large part to the pressures of the communist Polish government. They wanted to be intensely involved in the appointment of bishops to ensure there was no conflict with their communist agenda. Oddly enough, the government favored the appointment of Karol Wojtyła as the next archbishop and were prepared to turn down any other names. In their eyes, the young forty-two year old bishop of Kraków was a prime candidate, and the government officials thought he could be easily manipulated. As subsequent events would unfold, the government officials were proved completely wrong.

On March 8, 1964, Karol Wojtyła was officially installed as the Archbishop of Kraków. He became the spiritual leader of the ancient bishopric of Kraków; a successor to the great bishop Saint Stanisław who greatly helped further the Christianization of Poland and who became the first native saint of Poland. Karol Wojtyła looked to St. Stanisław for inspiration and intercession and beseeched his aid in shepherding the souls of Kraków. Wojtyła now possessed a great deal of responsibility at a very young age, but the energetic archbishop was up to the task. His youthful vigor helped him blaze a new trail in his archdiocese and continued to do so even after being named a cardinal.

Three years after his installation on June 28, 1967, Archbishop Wojtyła was elevated to the rank of cardinal. As a part of the "College of Cardinals," Wojtyła was initiated into a whole new world in the Catholic Church. He was now a close collaborator with the pope and was appointed various tasks to assist the Holy Father that required frequent visits to Rome. Yet, even though he was now recognized as a "Prince of the Church" and possessed one of the highest ranks in the Church hierarchy, he did not act like a medieval ruler who sat all day in his throne room. Instead, even as a cardinal, Wojtyła continued his ministry of "presence" and literally dwelt among his people. Besides traveling on a regular basis within the boundaries of his archdiocese, he hosted numerous conversations with a variety of men and women from all walks of life in his personal residence. Cardinal Wojtyła discussed intimate topics with actors, artists, philosophers, historians, musicians and writers, to name a few. He remained a man *of the people* and desired to serve their needs above all else. While he enjoyed being with the many faithful souls in the Archdiocese of Kraków, his charisma and ability to relate to the common man began to get noticed outside his native Poland.

On account of Karol Wojtyła's active role in the Second Vatican Council, as well as the strong rapport he had among the souls under his care, the young cardinal was greatly respected and well known among the upper levels of the Catholic Church hierarchy. Even Pope Paul VI took an interest in the Polish cardinal and treated him as a son. This close relationship was tangibly revealed when Pope Paul VI sent Wojtyła a generous gift of a stone from the tomb of Saint Peter. It was to be a part of the foundation for a new church built for laborers in Nowa Huta.[15] This simple action showed Wojtyła that the pope was near to him and his people and that the Successor of St. Peter was indeed a holy "father."

The Traveling Cardinal

It was not only the pope who took a special interest in the young cardinal. From the late-1960s through the mid-1970s, Cardinal Wojtyła was invited to visit Polish communities around the world. His first intense month of international travel led the Polish cardinal to Canada and the United States in 1969. Wojtyła visited numerous cities, the majority of them populated by Polish immigrants. In the United States he made stops in Buffalo, New York; Hartford and New Britain, Connecticut; Cleveland, Ohio; Pittsburgh, Pennsylvania; Detroit, Michigan; Boston, Massachusetts; Washington, D.C.; Baltimore, Maryland; St. Louis, Missouri; Chicago, Illinois; Philadelphia and Doylestown, Pennsylvania; and New York City, New York. In particular, he visited the Polish-American seminary in Orchard Lake, Michigan, and the Polish community known affectionately as the "American Częstochowa" in Doylestown, Pennsylvania. The Poles in the United States remained well-connected to their native land, and Cardinal Wojtyła was for them a revered and respected member of the Polish Catholic Church.

His relatively short whirlwind tour of the United States and Canada was only the beginning of his international ministry to Polish immigrants. The energetic cardinal, who at one time had never stepped foot outside of his native land, began to circumnavigate the world, visiting Polish communities wherever he went. In 1973, Cardinal Wojtyła made his longest trip away from Poland in order to participate in the Eucharistic Congress in Melbourne, Australia. Along the way Wojtyła made a pastoral visit to the Philippines and New Guinea, the latter being a destination of numerous Polish missionaries. He then made a handful of stops to Polish communities in Australia as well as New Zealand. Wojtyła took a special interest in the Polish people wherever they were in the world and saw himself as one of their shepherds. For Cardinal Wojtyła, the "diocese" in which he ministered no longer had any physical boundaries.

Eucharistic Congress in Philadelphia

Cardinal Wojtyła returned to the United States in 1976 when he was invited to give a homily at the International Eucharistic Congress in Philadelphia. The Congress went from August 1 through August 8 and proved to be a major event. The theme for the Congress was "The Eucharist and the Hungers of the Human Family." This theme was divided up into various topics, and Cardinal Wojtyła was asked to preach at a Mass on August 3 on the topic of "The Eucharist and Man's Hunger for Freedom." Other speakers at the conference included Dorothy Day, Mother Teresa and Archbishop Fulton J. Sheen. Suffice to say it was a monumental Congress, which was held during the 200th anniversary of the United States' founding. Even President Gerald Ford made an appearance, attending the closing Mass.

Before attending the Congress, in order to practice his English, Wojtyła stayed at the St. Sebastian Country Day School near Boston. He gave a lecture in Emerson Hall at Harvard and another at the Catholic University of America in Washington, D.C. He then returned to Philadelphia for the Congress. He took up residence at the St. Charles Borromeo Seminary and enjoyed speaking with the seminarians there.

Although the Eucharistic Congress was the reason for Cardinal Wojtyła's second visit of the United States, he took the opportunity to once again visit Polish communities. He traveled to Chicago and boarded a private jet (courtesy of Sentry Insurance), which flew him to rural Stevens Point, Wisconsin, for a brief respite in the countryside. It was there that Cardinal Wojtyła visited a historic community of Polish immigrants who remained close to their ancestral professions and created a "little Poland" in the heartland of America.

PART II

Cardinal Karol Wojtyła's Visit to Wisconsin

CHAPTER III

Polish Revival

There was a flurry of activity as Captain Stan Potocki stood attentively in the Sentry Apartments. Bishops and priests came in and out and clearly were trying to meet the needs of their honored guest. Potocki did not know much about the foreign dignitary. He knew the guest was a revered Polish cardinal who was invited to give a talk at the University of Wisconsin-Stevens Point. As the cardinal unpacked his belongings from the short flight between Chicago and Stevens Point, Potocki and another officer waited patiently for him in the apartment foyer. They had been assigned as his personal security guards and were entrusted with the task of ensuring the cardinal's safety during his brief visit to Wisconsin.

As the time came for the day's events to begin, Cardinal Karol Wojtyła and his personal secretary, Father Stanisław Dziwisz, walked into the foyer with Bishop Frederick Freking. As they exited the building, Cardinal Wojtyła stopped when he saw the two officers. He greeted them and gave a hard look at their name tags. Wojtyła noticed the name "Potocki" and slowly bowed towards the captain. Startled and confused, Stan wondered why of all people the cardinal was bowing to him! It should be the other way around! Cardinal Wojtyła asked Stan, "Do you know how revered your name is in Poland?" Oddly enough, Stan responded in the affirmative and told the cardinal that his grandfather was a mayor in Poland.

The Potocki family was renowned in Poland and originated in the area of Krakow, where Cardinal Wojtyła was Archbishop. Numerous political, military, and cultural leaders had come from the Potocki family and had played a vital role in the history of Poland. A few of Stan's ancestors immigrated to the United States and made their residence in a large rural Polish community in central Wisconsin. Stan had descended from noble lineage, and Cardinal Wojtyła knew it instantly when he saw the name. Wojtyła left the foyer accompanied by his entourage and continued on with the various activities of the day. One thing was sure: from the very beginning this Polish community made him feel right at home.[16]

A New Beginning

In the summer of 1857, the first Polish immigrants to central Wisconsin left their native land in Eastern Europe and traveled across the Atlantic to a new world brimming with opportunity. These immigrants from Poland were not alone in their desire for a better life as countless men and women made the journey to America in the nineteenth century. The vast majority of Polish immigrants made their residences in industrial cities across the United States. They were eager to be employed in factories so that they could send money back to their relatives who were still living under foreign occupation. Many hoped someday to rejoin their relatives after making enough money. Scholars have estimated that around one-quarter of these immigrants did in fact return home.[17]

For many Poles, life in a prosperous nation overflowing with opportunity was much more appealing than life in a land which technically did not exist. Since 1793 Poland had been wiped off the map and split up into three partitions, ruled separately by the Emperor of Austria, the King of Prussia, and the Empress of Russia. It was no surprise that being a second-class citizen with the potential of being drafted into a foreign military made numerous Polish men desire a fresh start in a "Land of Opportunity."

However, the Poles who traversed waterways and railways to reach their destination of central Wisconsin did not have any hopes of going back to their native land. Instead, they chose to make a new beginning in a place that already felt much like home.

"Little Poland"

By the time the first Polish settlers came to the area now known as Portage County, they were met by a small community of German immigrants. This encouraged them to settle there as many Poles had a working knowledge of the German language. It was not uncommon for Poles back home to work on German farms to gain extra income, so working alongside a German neighbor was familiar territory. What truly gave these poor Polish farmers the incentive to call Portage County home, however, was the inexpensive land. At the time, Wisconsin was still on the outskirts of the American frontier and was sparsely populated. These conditions resulted in Polish pioneers being able to purchase forty, eighty, or even 160 acres of untouched land with little money.[18] Back in Poland, only a nobleman could own that much land.

Consequently, the simple Polish farmers recognized the golden opportunity, bought land in Portage County, and set their hands to the plow. Many quickly made themselves at home and started to grow familiar crops such as rye and potatoes. In the off-season and winter months, the farmers sought work in the fast-growing logging industry of nearby counties. The extra work allowed the poor immigrants to have a steady income that supported their families.

The first Polish settlers to the area wrote to their relatives and friends back home and gave rave reviews of the land and opportunity for work. The settlers encouraged their relatives to make the arduous journey and join them in the frontier lands of Wisconsin. As a result, it did not take long for Portage County to be overrun by Polish immigrants. For example, the town of Sharon in Portage County began with one Polish family in 1857 and grew to over 2,000 inhabitants in the 1890s.[19] Almost all of the city's residents were first generation Polish immigrants. Family after family traveled to central Wisconsin, and soon Portage County became well known as a primary stop for rural Polish farmers. Several of the immigrants founded a town called "Polonia," affectionately known as "Little Poland."

The nearby city of Stevens Point also quickly began to attract new inhabitants on account of the new railroad and lumber industry. The Poles who chose not to farm were quick to find work in the growing city and became a major ethnic group alongside the Germans and Irish who were already there. The increasing number of Polish churches that sprang up in the rural countryside as well as in the burgeoning city of Stevens Point were a visible sign of the Polish presence. Wherever the Poles went, so went their Catholic faith.

To Be Polish Was To Be Catholic

Ever since the baptism of King Mieszko I in 966, the Polish people have remained firmly attached to the Christian religion. This was no different for the Poles who came to central Wisconsin. Wherever a group of Polish immigrants gathered, there a Catholic Church was built. By the early part of the twentieth century, Polish immigrants built nearly ten Catholic churches in a radius of 20 miles. They were led by numerous Catholic priests from Poland who came specifically to serve their needs. Catholicism was inextricably linked with their culture, and they simply could not live without a Catholic church.

To serve the needs of this growing community, several convents were also founded in the area. The Polish community in rural Polonia needed religious sisters to teach the increasing number of children. The pastor at Sacred Heart Parish, Father Joseph Dabrowski (who would later found the Saints Cyril and Methodius Seminary in Orchard Lake, Michigan), sent a letter to Kraków, Poland, to invite the Third Order Franciscan Sisters of St. Felix to send a handful of their sisters to central Wisconsin.[20] The sisters accepted the challenge and in 1874, five of them made the long, arduous journey and became the first Polish religious sisters in the United States. They quickly got to work and started a Polish school that attracted families from as far away as Milwaukee. They also built an orphanage that served for years to come the many homeless children in the region.

There was also a need for religious sisters to teach the children in the city of Stevens Point. The School Sisters of Notre Dame were first invited to teach at the parochial school of Saint Peter's, and were followed shortly thereafter by the School

Sisters of St. Francis. The Sisters of St. Francis came from a large German congregation of teaching sisters from Milwaukee. It was not an ideal situation, however, and a handful of Polish women from Stevens Point who entered the congregation underwent discrimination from their German superiors.[21] Instead of being assigned classrooms to teach, the Polish women were given tasks in the kitchen and trained to be housekeepers.[22] These women did not enter the convent to be full-time cooks, but felt a call from God to teach the young Polish children. As a result, six religious sisters left Milwaukee and, with the blessing of the bishop of Green Bay, founded a new congregation in Stevens Point, which was part of the Diocese of Green Bay at the time. They would first be known as the Polish Sisters of St. Joseph (later on to be known as simply the Sisters of St. Joseph) and quickly broke ground for their own motherhouse and academy for girls. Yet, even though the strong Polish Catholic culture was firmly established in central Wisconsin and was reinforced by the Polish religious sisters, it did not take long for the next generation to divert from the ways of their ancestors. As with many immigrant families during the early twentieth century, the young people of central Wisconsin desired to fit in with the culture and be more "American" than Polish.

Is Anyone Polish Anymore?

As the nineteenth century ended, the Polish community of Portage County continued to grow. Polish periodicals, newspapers, and grocery stores could be found in abundance. Polish life was thriving in central Wisconsin. The immigration of new Polish families steadily decreased. Those who were already there had settled down and were doing quite well. The local economy was booming. Those who dwelt in the city no longer found themselves impoverished. This new-found prosperity led to an increased number of farm children leaving their families in the country to pursue more affluent jobs in the city. Because of this mass exodus, the number of farms was cut in half between 1950 and 1970; new developments quickly overtook the outskirts of the city.[23] The urban area of Stevens Point expanded and began to encroach on the farms that were nearby.

Young people became less enthusiastic about the traditions of their parents, and many no longer valued their Polish roots. By the 1960s, instead of eating their mother's rye sandwich, teenagers began to prefer the new, cheap, and juicy McDonald's hamburger.[24] Not only did young people stop eating ethnic food, but even the Polish language ceased to be taught in area schools during the 1950s.[25] The loss of the language naturally led to the loss of culture. Polish priests were no longer sent to Stevens Point; the number of ordained clergy of Polish descent steadily dropped as the 1960s moved onward. Hymns at Mass were sparsely sung in Polish; there were few opportunities available to go to confession in Polish. Fewer people were proud of their Polish heritage; most preferred the ways of America to the outdated "Old World."

A small group of individuals noticed this trend and decided to do something about it. They saw that even though the Stevens Point area remained a place where a large portion of citizens were of Polish descent, few knew the Polish language or the culture of their ancestors. For most people, being Polish in Portage County simply meant that you had a Polish last name and ate pączki (read "special donuts") before Lent. Yet, there was one Polish couple who sought to change that attitude. They knew there had to be a "Polish Revival."[26]

Poles In Exile

In 1963, a man and his wife who had risked their lives to defend the Polish people arrived on the campus of the University of Wisconsin-Stevens Point. That couple was Dr. Waclav Soroka and his wife Zofia "Olenka" Soroka. Dr. Soroka was invited to teach Russian and East European history as a faculty member at UWSP. Dr. Soroka and his wife emigrated from Poland to the United States, where they attained US citizenship. Yet, it was not by choice that they left Poland. They were forced into exile by the communist government in Poland and were threatened with imprisonment and even death.

Back in Poland, both Waclav and Olenka were active members of the Polish armed resistance movement. They were members of the "Home Army" which was an underground resistance movement during the Nazi Occupation. Olenka served the "Home Army" in many different ways, which included

> "the role of military courier, traveling by train or small motorcycle, passing along classified communications among resistance centers. During the same time she participated in clandestine efforts to smuggle medicines and other assistance to Jewish inmates of the Majdanek concentration camp on the Lublin outskirts."[27]

Both members of the "Home Army," Waclav and Olenka met amidst their clandestine activities and were married by the end of the War. After the Nazi occupation, the Soviet Union stepped in with an occupation of their own. This did not bode well for the Sorokas, who were quickly forced into exile because of their opposition to Russian forces during the War. They left Poland and escaped to Western Europe, where they had three children over the next four years.

In 1954, the Soroka family made a final trip to the United States and first settled in Bloomington, Indiana, where Dr. Soroka studied and worked at Indiana University. Before finally coming to UWSP in 1963, Dr. Soroka led the Slavic section of the library at the University of Illinois at Urbana-Champaign. After the Sorokas arrived in Stevens Point, Olenka also worked at UWSP at the University Library and served there faithfully for many years.

Polish Revival

Both Dr. Soroka and his wife Olenka set out to foster Polish culture in central Wisconsin. They had risked their very lives for the Polish nation and knew first hand the importance of having a distinct culture. Additionally, the Sorokas were still very connected to Poland and wanted to shed more light on the plight of Poles living under Communist rule.

Dr. Soroka wanted to establish and expand Polish studies at the University as well as to expand the greater community's awareness of their Polish heritage and help produce pride in it. For example, Dr. Soroka visited a grade school and found the children timid to admit their Polish heritage. Few raised their hands when asked if any had Polish ancestors. Then Dr. Soroka proceeded to give the students a brief history lesson on Poland

and by the end almost all of the students raised their hands; they then knew what it meant to be Polish and were proud of their heritage.[28]

In 1968, Dr. Soroka also helped found a group called the Annual Lectures on Poland. This group was formed with the assistance of numerous community leaders, all of whom desired to bring a greater appreciation of Polish culture to Portage County. Several years later this group decided to take the "Polish Revival" to the next level and were bold enough to invite a Polish cardinal to come to central Wisconsin. Providentially there was a Polish cardinal adventurous enough to accept the invitation.

In 1975, the members of the Annual Lectures on Poland grew interested in the International Eucharistic Congress to be hosted in Philadelphia and received word that it would attract Catholics from all over Europe. They further discovered that a delegation of Polish bishops and priests were asked to attend the international gathering. This would facilitate a rare opportunity for Polish-Americans to experience a little bit of home and reconnect with their ancestors. Dr. Soroka saw this as a perfect chance to aid his endeavors to revitalize Polish culture in central Wisconsin and sought to invite an old friend to be a keynote speaker.

The Second Choice: The Other Polish Cardinal

Dr. Soroka invited Cardinal Stefan Wyszynski to be the keynote speaker at a special event hosted by the Annual Lectures on Poland, after the conclusion of the Eucharistic Congress. Unfortunately, Cardinal Wyszynski let Dr. Soroka know that he was unable to attend. He was not going to lead the delegation of

Polish bishops to the Eucharistic Congress, but suggested inviting the "other Polish cardinal"—Cardinal Karol Wojtyła. Cardinal Wyszynski knew that Wojtyła would be a good fit, and it was Wojtyła who would be leading the delegation of Polish bishops in Wyszynski's place.

Dr. Soroka changed plans and made arrangements to invite Cardinal Wojtyła. He accepted. However, Cardinal Wojtyła gave one condition; the Bishops of the United States needed to approve the plan. This turned out to be the first obstacle.

First Obstacle: US Bishop's Conference

As noted, the one condition that Cardinal Wojtyła gave to his visit to central Wisconsin was that it needed to receive the proper approval from the US Bishops. This idea did not gain instant approval.

Dr. Soroka immediately sought to contact Bishop Arthur Krawczak, a priest of Polish ancestry who was consecrated an auxiliary bishop of Detroit. Bishop Krawczak was involved with the itinerary of the Polish hierarchy coming to the United States for the Eucharistic Congress and acted as a representative of the US Conference of Bishops. He was very reluctant to approve such an invitation and tried to dissuade Dr. Soroka in making plans. According to Bishop Krawczak, there was little time for this type of excursion to a remote part of the country. It simply would take too long to fly out to Stevens Point, especially since it did not have a major airport. Bishop Krawczak told Dr. Soroka to back away from the request and not to pursue it. This did not deter Dr. Soroka, who assured the bishop that the matter was not closed. He would find another way.

Second Obstacle: Transportation

Dr. Soroka knew that there was one possibility that had not yet been examined: a private jet. A local insurance company, Sentry Insurance, had in their possession two private jets that would immediately solve the logistics problem. Dr. Soroka promptly contacted John Joanis, president of Sentry Insurance and beseeched him to allow the Annual Lectures on Poland to use one of their jets to fly in the Polish cardinal. It seemed like a long shot, but Dr. Soroka was determined to find a way to make his event a reality.

Providentially, Mr. Joanis' immediate response was, "yes." He would fly the cardinal from Chicago to Stevens Point and then to any location that the cardinal needed to go after the visit. There was, however, one more condition: the plan needed to be agreeable to Lee Sherman Dreyfus, the chancellor of the University in Stevens Point. This was troubling as the transportation of the cardinal was an urgent matter—the Eucharistic Congress was nearing its conclusion and the Polish bishops were already preparing to tour the United States. Seeing the urgency, Mr. Joanis approved the flight plan immediately (without consulting the chancellor) and Dr. Soroka left his office with a copy of the itinerary.

Dr. Soroka then called Bishop Krawczak and, to the bishop's surprise, relayed the recent development. The primary obstacle had been removed, and Cardinal Karol Wojtyła would be permitted to make a stop in Stevens Point, Wisconsin, among the many other cities he would visit that summer. Dr. Soroka decided to solidify the plans and flew to Orchard Lake, Michigan, to speak with Cardinal Wojtyła personally. Cardinal Wojtyła was visiting Michigan after the conclusion of the Eucharistic Congress in Philadelphia and confirmed the proposed program in Stevens Point. Everything appeared to be in order by August 15, a week before his scheduled appearance in Wisconsin.

There proved to be, however, one more transportation obstacle to his visit, which occurred a mere day before the cardinal's visit. All the arrangements were ready and, barring any catastrophe, the Polish cardinal would arrive in Stevens Point as scheduled. One day before his scheduled appearance in Wisconsin, auxiliary Bishop Alfred Abramowicz from Chicago, a friend of Cardinal Wojtyła, sought to delay his visit to Stevens Point. He called Dr. Soroka and explained to him how he wanted to organize a few events in Chicago for the cardinal to attend. This would require delaying the visit to central Wisconsin by a few hours.

Dr. Soroka refused.

It was one day before the scheduled events in Stevens Point and Dr. Soroka would not make more concessions. In fact, this attempt to further thwart the visit came at the end of what turned out to be a month of opposition leading up to the cardinal's visit. For many weeks Dr. Soroka had been sweating over the final logistical obstacle to the visit. It had to do with his proposed Mass on University grounds. While at first local university officials favored the public celebration of religion on the property of a state-sponsored university, those higher up did not have the same sentiment.

Third Obstacle: Separation of Church and State

The committee entrusted with organizing Cardinal Wojtyła's visit had ironed out every little detail. Leonard Groshek, a local state representative at the time, was appointed by the committee to be in charge of the itinerary and made sure the different events flowed seamlessly. The cardinal's visit was short, and so they had to take advantage of every minute he was here. Naturally there would be the public celebration of Mass and it was up to the committee to secure a venue.

Dr. Soroka was certain that because Cardinal Wojtyła was of such prominence in Poland and continued to hold much influence with the Polish people across the world, the Mass would attract thousands of Polish Catholics. In fact, the Annual Lectures on Poland expected 10,000 people to attend the celebration of Mass. There did not exist a church big enough to host such a gathering. The committee first sought to conduct an open air Mass on the top of the stairways in front of the College of Fine Arts. In the event of rain, the Mass would be moved to the Quandt Fieldhouse. The first and most obvious question that the chancellor of the University had was in regard to the "separation of Church and State." Did this infringe upon the Constitution of the United States or that of the State of Wisconsin?

The initial answer: no. It did not infringe upon either and the group was given permission to have the Mass on university property. That was, until the event needed the approval of the board of directors of the entire state university system. Particular members of the board did not like the idea of a Catholic cardinal celebrating a religious ceremony on university grounds. While there was nothing barring the event in the Constitutions, the board of directors did not want to proceed hastily and feared a backlash. The University then reversed its decision and told Dr. Soroka to find another venue.

And he did, oddly enough, on the grounds of a public high school. Dr. Soroka was able to gain permission to have Mass celebrated in the gymnasium of the newly built Stevens Point Area Senior High. The university couldn't allow the Mass, but the public high school saw no problem with it. Thus, all the obstacles were removed and the visit could go forward as planned.

Maurice Groshek Farm (Used with Permission)

Karol Wojtyła with Leonard & Regina Groshek
and Bishop Freking (Used with Permission)

Karol Wojtyła with Mary Jane Zdroik holding Christopher Buss (Courtesy of the Portage County Historical Society)

Karol Wojtyla fielding questions from local reporters at the Zdroik farm (Courtesy of the Portage County Historical Society)

Annual Lectures Pilgrimage Group with John Paul II at
Castel Gandolfo on June 5, 1980 (Used with Permission)

John Paul II with Maynard Zdroik at Castel Gandolfo
on June 5, 1980 (Used with Permission)

Annual Lectures Pilgrimage Group with John Paul II at
General Audience in St. Peter's Square (Used with Permission)

CHAPTER IV

The Green of America

As expected, Cardinal Karol Wojtyła and his personal secretary Father Stanisław Dziwisz arrived on the morning of August 23 at the small municipal airport in Stevens Point, Wisconsin, via a personal jet, courtesy of Sentry Insurance, from a short stop in Chicago. His plane touched down around 9:10 AM on Monday morning and the cardinal was greeted by a small group of representatives of the local community.

Among those who greeted him were Mrs. Jane Staples, a representative of Sentry Insurance, Zofia and Waclaw Soroka, and Leonard and Regina Groshek on behalf of the Annual Lectures on Poland. Additionally, Bishop Frederick Freking of the Diocese of La Crosse, and Father Chester Zielinski of Saint Peter Catholic Church greeted the Polish cardinal in the name of the Catholic communities of the area. The greeting party was also comprised of Dean John Nowak; Maynard and Mary Jane Zdroik; James Fiegelson, the mayor of Stevens Point, and his wife; additional representatives of the Annual Lectures on Poland; the Wisla Polish Dance Group; a company of Knights of Columbus members dressed in their finery; and a few other representatives of the local community. All in all it was a greeting befitting a highly revered foreign dignitary.

Many of the Poles who were present at the greeting also dressed in folk costumes typical of the Polish rural communities they descended from. This gave the Polish cardinal a sense of home, seeing familiar colors and embroidery that were very common across his native land. In fact, when he was a simple priest he took many vacations on a lake in Poland that was near a community of humble Polish farmers. This community of Gulcz, now the official "Sister City" of Stevens Point, was the place of origin for many families who settled in central Wisconsin. In a very real sense Cardinal Wojtyła was given a taste of home.

The official greeting of the Polish cardinal would not have been complete without the offering of bread and salt. The organizers of the event saw it a fit opportunity to revive a lost tradition of Polish hospitality. This ancient tradition of handing a guest the gift of bread and salt was practiced throughout Poland for many centuries. These two items were seen as "staples" in life and were given to guests to wish them good will. Generally speaking, this custom had diminished over the years, but was still seen in the ceremonies surrounding a traditional Polish wedding.

Not only was Cardinal Wojtyła given the "staples" of life, but also many gifts from the children present. The children offered the cardinal red roses and small flowers, and one child carried a small sheaf of wheat. Cardinal Wojtyła in turn showed his love and appreciation of the children's gifts and distributed holy cards to them. This meeting did not take too long, as the cardinal was on a tight schedule. At the conclusion of the greeting at the Stevens Point Municipal Airport, Cardinal Wojtyła entered into a car with Bishop Freking, driven by Chet Brilowski with Regina Groshek in the passenger seat. Wojtyła was followed by another car with Father Stanisław Dziwisz and Leonard Groshek, who made sure the itinerary he created was faithfully executed. The motorcade was escorted by local police to one of the oldest Polish congregations in the area, Saint Peter Catholic Church.

A New Parish For A Growing Polish Community

In the summer of 1860, Father John Polak was appointed to St. Stephen's Catholic Church in Stevens Point, "which was the only Catholic Congregation in Stevens Point, composed of Irish, French, German and a few Polish families."[29] Three years later in 1863 the Poles who settled outside of Stevens Point had greatly increased and needed to form another congregation of their own. These poor farmers were easily given approval to form a new parish, called St. Joseph's Church. However, once again this congregation was not able to serve the ever-increasing needs of the Polish community. More and more families began to populate the area, which meant another parish needed to be built. Polish families from Stevens Point attended St. Joseph's until 1876, at which point a new congregation was founded.

During that summer of 1876, Father Bogacki was sent to Stevens Point to help found a new church for Polish immigrants and assembled enough Polish families in the city to accomplish this task. He quickly raised the money to begin a new Polish church, which would be known as "St. Peter's." Thus began a new era in Stevens Point—St. Peter's would later become one of the largest Polish parishes in the area.

Home Away From Home

This history made Saint Peter's a fitting stop on Karol Wojtyła's tour of Portage County. The Polish atmosphere still permeated the congregation of Saint Peter's and made the young cardinal feel right at home. It was evident from his warm expressions and casual manner that he was among his kinsfolk. Wojtyła ascended the steps with Bishop Freking and entered the church to greet the congregation who were waiting for him. Everyone instantly fell in love with the cardinal as he could not help but hold and hug any children that came into his path. This truly was not your ordinary "Prince of the Church."

Upon reaching the front of the Church, Cardinal Wojtyła gave the traditional greeting of "The Lord be with you," while the congregation gave the appropriate response "vigorously in Polish." Feeling comfortable with the number of Poles inside Saint Peter's, Wojtyła gave a short address and said a few additional prayers in the Polish language. It was a brief stop, but Wojtyła still made time to talk with parishioners before he returned to the car and was led outside the city to visit area farms.

"The Green of America"

This part of the visit proved to be a highlight for the Polish Cardinal and was something Wojtyła specifically wanted to do. One of the main reasons why Cardinal Wojtyła was interested in coming to a rural area in Wisconsin was on account of his desire to see the "green of America."[30] He related to his hosts that "whenever he came to the United States all he ever saw was 'cement in cities' and he wanted to see where the Polish farmers lived."[31] Throughout his whole life Wojtyła preferred the hills and mountains of Poland, and every time he came to the United States he had been invited to large metropolitan cities and only saw massive cement skyscrapers or other commercial buildings. Additionally, Wojtyła wanted to escape the city so that he could tour rural Polish family farms. He was familiar with family farms back home and wanted to see how they operated in the United States. There were even a few native Poles working on the farms to be trained in different agricultural techniques to take back to Poland. Coming to central Wisconsin then was a treat, as he could breathe the rural fresh air that he loved so much and visit with Polish families. The organizers, therefore, made sure to include six farms on the itinerary.

His tour began around 10:30 AM and his first stop was at the dairy farm of Maurice Groshek. He greeted farmers there, toured the facilities, and blessed their home. Cardinal Wojtyła asked all sorts of questions about the equipment the farmers used. He asked Maurice if he could see how the "haylage unloader worked." Maurice proceeded to show him and quickly "dust came down the chute and scattered over him, but he didn't mind at all." Even Bishop Freking was impressed by this foreign cardinal and was surprised that the Prelate was not shaken or disgusted by what happened. Cardinal Wojtyła received first hand experience of farm life in Wisconsin. For someone who spent the summers kayaking and hiking the countryside of Poland, Wojtyła could not have been more at home.[32]

Before leaving for his next stop, Cardinal Wojtyła spoke with Maurice's son Frank and urged him to keep the tradition of farming alive. He then proceeded to visit the farm of Ed Zdroik, who recently had a stroke and was confined to his home. Cardinal

Wojtyła spent an extended amount of time speaking with Mr. Zdroik and gave him a special blessing. Throughout his life, Wojtyła had a special closeness and care for those who were suffering and sick and displayed this even during his short visit in Wisconsin.

After visiting with Ed Zdroik, Cardinal Wojtyła returned to his escort and was driven through an old Polish settlement area. Then the cardinal made a brief stop at the parish church, school, and rectory of Saint Adalbert in Rosholt. This parish also had rich Polish roots, similar to the history of Sacred Heart in Polonia, but was one of the more "recent" Polish churches when it opened its doors in 1898.

Picnic Lunch and Press Conference

To give the young cardinal a rest from the demands of the tour, he was led to the farm of Maynard and Mary Jane Zdroik. The Zdroik family did not know what to expect when Cardinal Wojtyła visited their potato farm outside of Stevens Point. They knew he was a prominent and youthful cardinal in Poland, but they never met him personally before he came to central Wisconsin. Upon his arrival, they quickly discovered that the cardinal was an avid outdoorsman and fearless adventurer. What surprised them most was his effortless ability to climb at age fifty-six.

Portage County is generally known as a flat area with little change in elevation. It is often referred to as a plains area and is a mixture of agricultural fields and thick forests. Wojtyła had a knack for finding the highest place in a given area in order to survey it. As a result, when he noticed that the highest point on the farm was the silo, he naturally asked if he could scale it. The

Zdroiks, especially the boys of the farm, were quite surprised by the request and at the same time impressed. They had never seen a Catholic priest, much less a cardinal dressed in his black cassock with a golden pectoral cross hanging around his neck, scale a silo. Yet, his clerical garb did not deter him, and Cardinal Wojtyła climbed the vertical ladder with relative ease, reached the top of the tower, and gazed over the vast plains below. He wanted to see the "green of America," and that is exactly what he saw.[33]

Mary Janc prepared a sumptuous picnic lunch for about 150 people with all kinds of Polish food. Since they did not have enough room in their home, the lunch was set-up outside on their front lawn. Among the distinguished guests were Chancellor Dreyfus of UWSP and John Joanis of Sentry Insurance. Mary Jane offered Cardinal Wojtyła tea or coffee, and instead he simply asked for water.[34] He visited with everyone who was there, and all felt like they were talking to an old friend.

Afterwards, there was a press conference at the farm with numerous reporters, including a local TV news crew. During the conference the reporters asked him a variety of questions and some even dared to question him about the political situation in Poland. Wojtyła sternly rebuked the reporter and refused to comment on the communist government and the tense situation in his homeland, chastising the reporter for not knowing his politics. Nevertheless, he continued his tradition of shaking everyone's hands and picking up any child he could see. He was extremely pleased with his visit to the farm and extended an invitation to Maynard and Mary Jane to visit him in Kraków.

Concluding his visit of the Zdroik farm, he proceeded to visit the Lakeview Farms, the Stanislawski Farms, and the Eugene Zdroik Farm. To finish his tour of rural Wisconsin, he visited

Sacred Heart Church in Polonia, including the school and rectory, as well as the Felician sisters who were stationed there. This proved to be another important stop for Cardinal Wojtyła as he had a close relationship with the Felician order. The official name of the religious order is Zgromadzenie Sióstr św. Feliksa z Kantalicjo (Sisters of St. Felix of Cantalice), and are most commonly known as the "Felician Sisters."

A Familiar Religious Order

The Felicians were founded by Blessed Mary Angela Truszkowska in 1855 in Warsaw, Poland, and soon after in 1869 were called to move their motherhouse to Kraków. Blessed Mary Angela had a special devotion to St. Felix of Cantalice, a Capuchin Franciscan who had a particular love and attention to children. St. Felix was a personal friend of St. Philip Neri and led an active-contemplative life teaching children in Rome. Thus, she named her congregation of sisters after St. Felix and began to devote her entire life not only to the forgotten children of Poland, but also the less fortunate and homeless of the city.

Quickly after the founding of the Felician Sisters, they were asked to minister to the needs of rural children throughout Poland. They did this very successfully and were well known for their good work. As a result, it was no surprise when the pastor at Sacred Heart Parish in Polonia, Father Joseph Dabrowski, sent a letter to Kraków to invite the Sisters of St. Felix to send a few of their sisters from Poland to central Wisconsin. The sisters accepted the challenge and became the first Polish religious sisters in the United States. As they left Kraków, they were given a blessing by Blessed Mary Angela Truszkowska, who heartily approved the new mission. The Sisters quickly got to work and started a Polish school that would attract families from all over Wisconsin and built an orphanage that served homeless children in the region. Thus, the Sisters in Polonia had a direct connection to Kraków and to Blessed Mary Angela.

Special Connection

Cardinal Karol Wojtyła, as Archbishop of Kraków, knew the Felician Sisters very well and would often visit with them in his home diocese. While in Rome, he asked the Felicians there to drive him to his various appointments around the Eternal City.[35] Over the years Wojtyła became well acquainted with the order and appreciated their ministry to the orphans and homeless. All of this familiarity eventually led him to beatify Mary Angela Truszkowska in 1993 after he became Pope John Paul II. For Wojtyła, coming to central Wisconsin to visit the first foundation of Felician Sisters in North America was something personal and further confirmed his appreciation of the Felician order. His own affection and love for children remained dear to his heart and the Felician Sisters gave a tangible expression of that love in their apostolate.

Thus far the day that was planned for the Polish cardinal proved to be a pleasant treat. For Cardinal Wojtyła, speaking to a Polish congregation, visiting a beautiful countryside, and greeting a familiar religious order reminded him of home, and he could not help but feel close to the people he met. Next he had to return to the city and deliver the lecture for which he had been invited.

CHAPTER V

Catholic Education in Poland

When Dr. Arthur Herman received an invitation to attend a banquet at the University Center, he didn't think much of it. From what he understood, a Catholic cardinal from Poland was going to give a lecture. All he knew about the cardinal was that he served as a professor of philosophy at the University of Lublin and was a well-known philosopher in Poland. At the very least he held this in common with the Polish cardinal, as Professor Herman was a philosopher and was recently asked to be the chair of the philosophy department at the University of Wisconsin-Stevens Point. Nevertheless, it was a University-sponsored event and the organizers had specifically asked him to attend, so he accepted the invitation.

Upon arrival, Professor Herman was shocked to see that the University Center was packed. There wasn't an open seat to be found, and he did not recognize anyone who was there. Since he was invited to this banquet, there was a seat reserved for him on the floor of the hall, immediately in front of the head table. Professor Herman took his place and greeted those who were seated at his table.

As he did not know anyone present at the banquet, the philosophy professor decided to make conversation with the priest seated next to him. It was quickly evident that this priest had come to the event with the Polish cardinal and was his personal secretary, Father Stanisław Dziwisz [currently the Archbishop of Kraków]. The priest did not know much English and so Professor Herman decided to speak with him in a different language he knew: German. They continued to talk together for a time before the evening's events started. After a time of friendly conversation, Herman saw the printed program on the table and flipped it over to the blank side on the back. He proceeded to draw a small grid and placed a circle in one of the boxes. The philosophy professor passed the program to the Polish priest and was curious to see what would happen. The priest's eyes lit up as he took out his pencil and placed an "x" on a different box on the grid. The priest and professor continued to play numerous games of "Tic-Tac-Toe" until Herman looked again at the banquet's program. He noticed something that startled him; he was slated to give a welcoming address to the cardinal! As he looked up, he knew he would be asked to come forward in a few minutes and so he quickly formulated something to say in his head.

After an introduction of the honored guest by the Master of Ceremonies Roy Shafranski and a welcome address by Dr. Lee Sherman Dreyfus, the Chancellor of the University, Dr. Arthur Herman rose from his seat and gave his own address, welcoming a fellow philosophy professor. Herman delivered his quickly composed speech, directing it to the Polish cardinal. He joked that after the cardinal leaves America, he would have to deal with the many troubles of "Roman Catholicism." Professor Herman knew that Wojtyła, being a cardinal, would spend a lot of time in the city of Rome, and at first the Polish Prelate nodded with a smile, agreeing that there are unique challenges being a member of the Roman curia. Yet, Herman went further. He proceeded to emphasize that the cardinal would be faced with the many differences between "Roman Catholicism" and "American Catholicism." He intentionally made it known that he believed there were two different "types" of Catholicism in the Church—Herman knew that as a philosopher the cardinal would appreciate distinctions and definitions. Professor Herman's remarks were kept short and he did not go further into what were the primary differences of the two "types" of Catholicism. Dr. Waclaw Soroka then stepped forward and gave the final introduction to Cardinal Karol Wojtyła.

Professor Herman returned to his seat and listened attentively to the lecture by Cardinal Wojtyła. After Wojtyła's academic talk, Herman stayed around for a time and soon realized that the Polish cardinal wanted to speak with him. Fellow philosopher Cardinal Wojtyła walked over to Herman and thanked him for the welcoming address. Then he asked him to speak more specifically about the differences between what he called "Roman Catholics" and "American Catholics." Professor Herman proceeded to relate how there were differences on Catholics' views concerning priestly celibacy, abortion, marriage and divorce, to name a few. Herman noticed that Cardinal Wojtyła was intensely interested in the topic and continued to speak with him for over fifteen minutes. From Herman's perspective, Wojtyła did not appear rushed and desired only to talk with him. Cardinal Wojtyła was clearly interested in this topic as it was not a distinction he would have naturally been familiar with. In the back of his mind the Polish Prelate would have known that the truths of the Catholic Church do not change from country to country and are the same for everyone. Yet, even though Wojtyła would have disagreed with the distinction, the cardinal remained pleasant and open and smiled throughout his conversation. It appeared to Herman that he was the only person that Wojtyła wanted to talk to, although his organizers continually advised him to speed things up so that he would not be late for his next appointment. The Polish cardinal did not budge and only when he realized he needed to celebrate Mass at the local high school did he leave his personal conversation with Dr. Herman. In the eyes of Wojtyła, it was as if Dr. Herman was the only person in the room.[36]

An Academic Lecture

Originally the lecture at the University of Wisconsin-Stevens Point was to be called "The Situation of the Catholic Church in Poland," and no doubt was meant to highlight the many struggles of the Catholic Church in the communist country. Cardinal Wojtyła did not want to place undue attention on the situation of the Church in what was a very tumultuous situation. However, he did integrate into his talk some of the problems the Church faced with an atheistic government, but focused more on a general topic of "Catholic Learning in Poland."

His lecture was composed of four parts: An Introduction, A Historical Overview of Institutions and Structures, Some Fields of Catholic Learning in Poland, and Concluding Characteristics. The essence of his talk was a summary of Catholic education throughout the centuries, highlighting the many institutions that have been founded over the years.

At the end, he did give some commentary on the current state of Catholic education. For example, he stated how there is a tendency to reduce the influence of Catholic education and that this tendency flows from the "assumptions of an atheistic system, according to which religion in the new government ought to disappear, and if religion, then also theology and Catholic learning in general." He further expressed how the Church was trying to resist disappearing from mainstream education and "[did] not want to be confined to circles of professionals only." At that point in Poland's history, the communist government had taken religion out of all the schools, and religious instruction was no longer a part of the main curriculum.

Disappointment

Unfortunately, Cardinal Wojtyła's lecture focused almost entirely on the historical nature of Catholic education and was meant to be delivered to a room full of academics. The room only contained a handful of scholars and primarily contained local farmers and businessmen. As a result, the talk did not resonate with the crowd. Even Cardinal Wojtyła expressed disappointment with his talk and felt that he delivered a lecture much more suited to a room full of University faculty rather than to the simple men and women who were present.[37]

However, many of the attendees were impressed when he came around and greeted everyone. He had such a warm and inviting presence and was very approachable. In his opening address, Chancellor Dreyfus mentioned to the cardinal that he thought he could be the next pope if a non-Italian was ever chosen. Dreyfus introduced Wojtyła saying, "And here is the next pope of the Catholic Church." Cardinal Wojtyła shook his finger at Dreyfus and said, "If I become the next pope, you will become the next governor of Wisconsin!" The room roared with laughter at the jest that each of them made. Little did they know that two years later Wojtyła would be elected the 264th pope and a few months after, Lee Sherman Dreyfus was elected the fortieth governor of Wisconsin.

CHAPTER VI

Food for the Journey

The high school gymnasium was packed. Seating for the unique event included both sides of the bleachers as well as several rows of seats on the basketball court of the gym. Typically the gym would have been filled with cheering fans, rooting for the SPASH Panthers, praying that they would beat the opposing foe. This time, however, it was filled with men and women of all ages, some dressed in strange clothes, offering up a sacrifice to the Triune God. There was nothing ordinary about it.

Numerous fourth degree members of the Knights of Columbus were present to be the "honor guard" for the cardinal and were dressed in all their finery, swords in hand. Other members of the congregation wore their authentic Polish folk dress and some of them were asked to bring the bread and wine to the altar during the offertory. Many priests were present to concelebrate the Holy Sacrifice of the Mass with Cardinal Wojtyła on a portable altar. This altar was on loan from an area parish and was surrounded by six tall candlesticks atop a stage in the middle of the gym floor. Yet this entire setting was not what changed one man's life forever.

Reverend Conrad Kimbrough had been an Episcopalian priest for over twenty-five years. His latest post was at the Episcopal Church of the Intercession and recently he had become very dissatisfied with his ever-changing religion. In fact, it seemed to Kimbrough that too much was being changed. The General Convention recently switched its views on abortion, marriage laws, and began to ordain women as Episcopal priests. For Rev. Kimbrough, something had to give. So he decided to go on pilgrimage to ask God what he must do.

He flew over to Ireland and climbed the famous pilgrimage site of Croagh Patrick. There, atop the mountain upon which Saint Patrick had fasted and prayed for forty days, the Episcopalian priest cried out to God and beseeched Him to reveal His will. Kimbrough needed to know what God was calling him to do with his life. By the time he reached the bottom of Croagh Patrick, he knew what he needed to do. He was going to become Catholic.

Yet, Kimbrough still needed a sign from God to know that it was His will. Upon returning to his post in central Wisconsin, he was cordially invited to attend a banquet at the University that featured a visiting Polish cardinal. A good friend of his invited him to the lecture, and after the conclusion of the dinner Kimbrough was able to meet the cardinal who gave the talk. After a short conversation, Kimbrough was also invited to the Catholic Mass to be celebrated at the local high school that evening. Not knowing exactly where to sit in the large gymnasium, the Episcopalian priest scaled the bleachers and sat near the top. Still wearing his clerical collar, Kimbrough respected the traditions of the Catholic faith and knew that he could not receive Communion at the Mass. However, just like Zacchaeus, Rev. Kimbrough was asked to come down.

At the conclusion of the liturgy the priests and bishops formed a procession and began to leave the altar. Cardinal Wojtyła motioned to Bishop Freking, who in turn signaled Rev. Kimbrough and called out, "Father Kimbrough, come down!" Bishop Freking allowed Kimbrough to walk down the bleachers and directed him to stand in front of the cardinal. Karol Wojtyła then proceeded to utter a special blessing over the head of the Episcopalian priest. Kimbrough left that night a changed man and a few months later he converted to the Catholic Church and returned to his native North Carolina. The bishop in North Carolina instructed Kimbrough to report to seminary. Shortly thereafter he was ordained a Catholic priest. Father Conrad Kimbrough served an additional thirty-three years as a priest and inspired at least nine men to discern the call to the priesthood and two women to discern the call to religious life. That night in the gymnasium was the catalyst that changed his life forever.[38]

·············——————— ———————··········

One Body in Christ

The celebration of Mass by Cardinal Karol Wojtyła at the public high school proved to be a highlight for many area Catholics. This was a rare chance to participate in a Mass with a "Prince of the Church" and so it brought together not only Catholics of Polish decent, but also any Catholics in the area who were free to attend. The high school gym was packed with seating both on the floor as well as in the bleachers. Undoubtedly this was the first Mass ever to be celebrated in the public school gymnasium.

Among the clergy present for this unique Mass was Msgr. Zdzisław Peszkowski, a professor at the Seminary of Saints Cyril and Methodius in Orchard Lake, Michigan. Msgr. Peszkowski was a dear friend of Cardinal Wojtyła and was living in exile in the

United States. He had survived the Katyn Forest Massacre, where 22,000 Polish officers, civil servants, priests, teachers, and other Polish leaders were executed by the Soviets.[39] While Wojtyła toured the United States, Msgr. Peszkowski accompanied him and provided any assistance he could. Peszkowski was familiar with Wisconsin as he previously studied Polish literature at the University of Wisconsin-Madison in the 1960s.[40]

The music was provided by a joint effort of the area parishes. All the choirs were invited to come and lend their voices and were directed to sing numerous Polish hymns. As the Annual Lectures on Poland organized the entire day, it was fitting that the celebration of Mass be focused on the Polish heritage of the local citizens. This is also why it made sense to have the offertory brought up by a group of Poles dressed in the traditional garb of their ancestors. The Mass served as a public affirmation of authentic Polish culture, which at its heart was intimately tied to the Catholic Church.

Nevertheless, even though the Mass focused on Polish culture, the actual celebration was a mix of three different languages. The recitation of the Creed and the proclamation of the readings were in English, while the entire Mass was celebrated by Cardinal Wojtyła in the universal language of the Church: Latin. In fact, the only Polish prayer recited during the liturgy was the Ojcze Nasz (Our Father).[41]

Recognizing the opportunity to speak his native language, the cardinal chose to deliver his homily both in English and in Polish. Most of the congregation was not fluent in their ancestral language, but there were several participants who retained their memory of Polish and were transported back to their native land. In his homily, he "stressed the Eucharistic Congress as a unifying factor among people."[42] The cardinal had just spent several days in Philadelphia at the Eucharistic Congress and so it remained fresh in his mind. He had witnessed the coming together of people from all parts of the globe and recognized that the Congress unified a large variety of people from every race and nation. Later on as Pope John Paul II, Wojtyła issued an encyclical letter entitled *Ecclesia de Eucharistia* where he expanded upon this theme of unity and explained how, "Eucharistic communion … confirms the Church in her unity as the body of Christ [and] fulfills the yearning for fraternal unity deeply rooted in the human heart."[43]

Cardinal Wojtyła also tied together these two themes of unity and the reality of the Eucharist as the fulfillment of man's deepest longings at the Eucharistic Congress. While at the Congress, Wojtyła gave a homily at Veterans Stadium to a large crowd, during which he focused on the hunger of man for freedom and how the Eucharist is at the heart of every man's hunger. He proclaimed in Philadelphia,

> "The Eucharist is the food which satisfies man's deepest hunger. Created in the image and likeness of God himself (Gen 1:26), man can find the final appeasement of his hunger and fulfillment of his desires in God alone. 'Our heart is not quiet until it rests in Thee' (St. Augustine, Confessions I, 1).

> The Eucharist is the chief source of the wealth contained in the human heart. For God, who in this Sacrament 'gives himself wholly to us', through this spiritual Communion enriches man most magnificently and brings out from the

secret of man's heart all the treasures which its Creator has enclosed in it."[44]

In the high school gymnasium of SPASH, Cardinal Wojtyła wove these various themes into his homily and made them relevant to the particular community that was present at the celebration.

After Mass, the rather jovial and approachable cardinal impressed everyone. In fact, those who were present recounted, "He shook so many hands he could have been the President of the United States or the Pope."[45] Additionally, participants saw "a human quality about him ... and a lack of phoniness and pomp."[46] To the simple farmers of central Wisconsin he was not a cardinal who presumed himself greater than the people but seemed like one of them and was truly interested in who they were.

The next day, after spending the night in the Sentry Apartments, Cardinal Wojtyła concelebrated Mass at St. Joseph's Convent. He was invited to stay and eat breakfast with the Sisters of Saint Joseph and then visited two nursing homes: River Pines Community Health Center and the Portage County Home. This part of his trip was very unique and was a personal request of the cardinal. As the Archbishop of Kraków he often visited the sick and aging throughout the diocese. He saw being present to those who were suffering as a central part of his ministry and believed that their prayers and sacrifices gave him vitality as well. One day, after celebrating Mass at the chapel of the Daughters of Charity of St. Vincent de Paul in Kraków, Archbishop Wojtyła visited those in the infirmary where he said to them,

"Although I am young and strong, although I fly in airplanes, climb mountains, ski, I still turn to the weakest, so that by the riches of their suffering they may bring down the strength and power of the Holy Spirit and the blessing of God upon my work in the Archdiocese."[47]

After giving a joint blessing with Bishop Freking of the aged at the two homes, Cardinal Wojtyła arrived at the airport and boarded the Sentry Insurance private jet once again. He bade farewell to those present and was flown out to Boston "where he [was] to work on a philosophy book he [was] writing."[48] For Wojtyła, not only did he receive "food for the journey" in the celebration of Holy Mass, but also from the prayers and sufferings that the elderly of Portage County would now offer up for him during their final days on earth. In a certain sense, visiting the nursing homes was one of the most important actions he did while in central Wisconsin.

CHAPTER VII

Departing for a Far Away Country

At the conclusion of his visit to central Wisconsin, Cardinal Wojtyła was flown again by private jet to his next destination. Wojtyła landed in Boston, but then traveled to Pomfret, Vermont to spend a few days writing a philosophy book with Anna-Teresa Tymieniecka and relaxing with her family.[49] Together they worked on the English translation of his philosophical work, *Osoba i Czyn*, which previously had been published in Poland in 1969. The short time they spent in the quiet and solitude of the wilderness was very fruitful and in 1979 Tymieniecka published the translation under the title of "The Acting Person." Wojtyła then returned to Boston and flew out to San Francisco and Los Angeles and continued his tour of several Polish communities. After a few days on the West Coast, he again boarded a plane and visited Great Falls and Geyser, Montana, where he visited a dear priest friend of his from the Archdiocese of Kraków who had survived the Nazi Concentration Camps. Then Cardinal Wojtyła flew back to Chicago and then to Cincinnati to visit with the president of the US Bishop's Conference, Cardinal Joseph Bernadin. After a brief visit and a concelebrated Mass with Cardinal Bernadin, Cardinal Wojtyła visited the Polish Seminary in Orchard Lake, Michigan for a second time, and made a last trip to New York before heading off to Rome on his way back to Poland. All in all, Cardinal Wojtyła's visit to the United States was filled to the brim—it seemed like he visited every sizable Polish community in America!

At the conclusion of the visit the Polish cardinal was starting to raise eyebrows at the international level and continued to be revered by all Poles both in and outside of Poland. More and more people, including priests, bishops, and lay faithful, were becoming familiar with the youthful Archbishop of Kraków and recognized his charismatic personality and zeal for the Gospel. Yet, little did anyone know that in two years he would be given an even greater platform to proclaim the Gospel; and not only to Polish people.

After Karol Wojtyła's coast-to-coast tour of the United States in 1976, the Polish cardinal returned to his native land to continue the fight for a free Poland. This was an ongoing battle for Wojtyła ever since the communists took over power after World War II. Especially as a cardinal, Wojtyła was closely watched by the authorities to make sure he fell in line and did not incite revolt among the people. His apartment was bugged and under constant surveillance and his car was almost always followed. If the communists wanted to send an even clearer sign, they would beat up a priest of his archdiocese. Nevertheless, this did not deter the young cardinal, who continued to fight for his people and inspire them to retain their dignity as human persons.

An Aging Pope

At the same time, Pope Paul VI was feeling the burden of old age and began making provisions for his successor. Six years earlier in 1970, Paul VI, at the age of seventy-two, made several changes to the process of electing a new pope. For example, he made it a rule that all cardinals over eighty would no longer be able to vote in a papal conclave, thereby putting the future of the Church in the hands of younger cardinals.[50] Additionally, he set the maximum amount of papal electors to 120 cardinals.[51] Last of all, Paul VI made an attempt to curb the influence of older cardinals who might try to sway the electors by insisting on secrecy during the conclave.[52] The younger cardinals were the future of the Church, and Paul VI knew that one of them would succeed him.

Then it all happened. On August 6, 1978, on the feast of the Transfiguration, Paul VI died of a heart attack at his summer residence in Castel Gandolfo at the age of eighty. His death was not unexpected, as his health had been deteriorating gradually over time and with increasing rapidity in the last few months before his death. This meant that the College of Cardinals had already been discussing who would become his successor. Paul VI's legacy remained the Second Vatican Council and so the cardinals knew that the next pope should carry on the work of implementing the Council. Additionally, they began to look for cardinals who were more akin to Pope John XXIII's warm disposition, able to deliver the truth in a pastoral manner. However, Cardinal Wojtyła refused to speculate and completely trusted in the Holy Spirit's directives.

Wojtyła received news of the Pope's death while returning from vacation on August 8 and then proceeded to pack up his bags and leave for Rome on August 11. The young cardinal would participate in his first conclave to elect the next successor of St. Peter.

The Two Conclaves

After completing the papal funeral rites, the first conclave to elect the next pope began on August 25, 1978. What happened next was the fastest conclave since 1938 when at the time Pius XII was elected on the first day of voting. Cardinal Albino Luciani, Patriarch of Venice, was elected to the Chair of St. Peter on the fourth ballot on the first day of voting, August 26, the feast of Our Lady of Częstochowa, Queen of Poland. The cardinals wasted little time discovering whom God had chosen and everyone present at the conclave knew that Luciani was the man the Holy Spirit wanted in the Chair of St. Peter.

Luciani was a joy-filled cardinal, whom everyone was pleased to have met. In fact, Cardinal Wojtyła conversed with him on several occasions, even meeting him for lunch prior to the start of the conclave. Both cardinals shared much in common, including an unspoken spiritual connection. That is why it was with great sadness Cardinal Wojtyła returned to Rome thirty-three days later for the second conclave. Cardinal Luciani was installed as Supreme Pontiff on September 3, 1978 and took the name Pope John Paul I. He took this name in honor of his two predecessors, Pope John XXIII and Pope Paul VI and was the first pope in history to have a double name. Prophetically he chose the name "John Paul the First," knowing that his pontificate would end shortly after it began.

A mere thirty-three days after being elected, Pope John Paul I died unexpectedly on September 28, 1978. The world was shocked and Italians were stunned that their beloved "Smiling Pope" had passed away so soon after becoming their Shepherd. Cardinal Wojtyła received word about his death while at tea in his apartment. He proceeded straight to the chapel to pray for the repose of his soul as well as to ask the Lord why this had happened. Visibly shaken by the events, Cardinal Wojtyła again packed his bags and returned to Rome on October 3, 1978. It appeared that the young Cardinal may have been worried that he would be the one to replace John Paul I. In fact, many cardinals and curia members were already talking about Wojtyła as a possible candidate, while the Polish people were praying that he did not get elected. They loved him too much to see him leave his native land.

Even though it had been widely discussed as a possibility, the world was still surprised when, after the fourth ballot on October 16, 1978, a cardinal from a "far country" stepped out onto the balcony. When hearing his name many immediately thought the new Pope was an "African," not fully understanding the Polish last name. Cardinal Wojtyła became the first non-Italian pope in over 400 years.

He is in Rome

At about the same time that Karol Wojtyła was attending the second conclave, Maynard and Mary Jane Zdroik disembarked after their long flight from Wisconsin to Poland. They arrived in Poland after responding to an invitation extended by Cardinal Wojtyła to visit him at his residence in Kraków. He thoroughly enjoyed their company and hospitality during his visit in 1976 and so before he left central Wisconsin, Wojtyła invited them to visit him in Poland. Such a personal invitation from a high-ranking cardinal was a rare opportunity for the Zdroiks, and so they could not pass it up. Two years after his visit to their Polish farm they were able to make the long journey to the land of their ancestors.

The Zdroiks left the airport in Kraków and made their way to ul. Franciszkańska 3, knocking on the door of the Bishop's Palace. A priest greeted Maynard and Mary Jane at the door and led them to Cardinal Wojtyła's office. Expecting a warm greeting from an old friend, they were surprised to see that his office was empty besides one of the cardinal's secretaries. Maynard and Mary Jane were then instructed that their friend was not in Poland. Even though their visit had been scheduled months in advance and the Zdroiks flew thousands of miles to visit the cardinal, he wasn't even in the same country. In fact, he was in Rome and had a new name: Pope John Paul II.[53]

A Friend in the Vatican

For Poles back in central Wisconsin, the news of Wojtyła's election brought an enormous amount of pride and joy. John Paul II was not a distant pope, who no one knew, but a dear friend. The church bells sang loudly in Stevens Point and relatives called each other to share the great news. As far as Independence, Wisconsin, at the historically Polish parish of Saints Peter and Paul, the church bells rang loudly for at least half an hour. It was a proud day to be Polish, and there was much celebration throughout the region.

Shortly after his papacy began, those who met John Paul II in 1976 sought to visit their old friend in his new environment. One of the first groups from central Wisconsin to secure an audience with him in Rome was, not surprisingly, the Annual Lectures on Poland. About thirty pilgrims were part of this group, which included among others Olenka Soroka, James Cooper, and Maynard and Mary Jane Zdroik. Waclaw, who was himself unable to attend, was aided by Konstanty Turowski in making the necessary arrangements to secure a private audience for the group with John Paul II at his summer residence of Castel Gandolfo on June 5, 1980.[54]

The audience was a joyous occasion and had a familial quality. Before having the privilege to speak directly to the Holy Father, all those present (about 250, almost all of them from Poland) participated in a festive Corpus Christi Mass and procession.[55] During his homily, John Paul II commented on how it was such a joyous occasion for him to celebrate Corpus Christi with a "Polish heart."[56] He commented that the celebration reminded him how his "heart, first as a boy and then as a youth and then as a priest and then as a bishop, participated in this wonderful tradition of the 'Polish heart', that which for centuries felt that gratitude belonged to God for the Eucharist."[57] The gathering of Polish friends also reminded him of his visit to Poland the previous year, where he spent time in "Moglia, in Nowa Huta, in Kalwaria Zebrzydowska and also in other places."[58] All in all, it was a celebration he thoroughly enjoyed.

At the conclusion of the Mass, the group was ushered in to greet the Holy Father along with a separate group of Polish pilgrims. The private audience was about an hour long and after speaking with everyone, John Paul II invited the large group to stay for lunch. He wanted to repay both the Annual Lectures on Poland for hosting him as well as the Zdroiks for the wonderful meal he had on their front lawn in Rosholt and even commented on how good the kielbasa was that they cooked for him.[59] The impromptu lunch, however, was arranged too quickly for the papal cooks and the group from Wisconsin was not sure if there would be enough food for everyone. Mary Jane looked at the Polish pilgrims, who dearly loved their native son, and suggested that they decline the invitation so that John Paul II could have an intimate lunch with his fellow countrymen.

Another way that John Paul II remained close to central Wisconsin was by his support of an orphanage in Peru started by Father Joseph Walijewski. Father Walijewski was a Polish priest of the Diocese of La Crosse and served as an associate at Saint Peter Catholic Church in Stevens Point from July 3, 1951, until September 5, 1956. He was accepted into the Diocese on account of his Polish heritage because central Wisconsin needed more priests who could speak the language. Later on Father Joe Walijewski was granted permission to dedicate his life to the missions in South America and desired to start an orphanage there. After John Paul II became pope in 1978, Father Joe heard that he would be making a visit to his native land of Poland and desired to meet him there. During the historic days of June 2-10, 1979, Father Joe spoke with John Paul II and related to him the poverty that existed in Peru. Father Walijewski was even bold enough to invite him there to see it. Six years later John Paul II accepted the invitation and met again with Father Joe during his papal visit to Peru. John Paul II saw the utter poverty the people of Peru were living in and was quick to leave $50,000, which was directed to Father Joe. That generous donation of John Paul II paved the way for a new orphanage in Peru and Father Joe named it "Casa – Hogar Juan Pablo II," which is translated "House – Home of John Paul II." The orphanage has been a mission of the Diocese of La Crosse ever since and the cause of beatification and canonization for Father Joseph Walijewski was recently opened in 2013.[60]

Worldwide Celebrity

As his papacy progressed, it became clear that while John Paul II dearly loved his Polish countrymen and enjoyed ministering to their needs, his new mission was to evangelize the entire world. This he accomplished like no other Pope before him. John Paul II visited more than 125 countries, traveling 680,000 miles by the end of his twenty-six year pontificate.[61]

Wherever he traveled he sought to speak in the native language of the people and speak to them in their cultural context. Speaking in this way increased his ability to connect to all people and allowed him to break down any cultural barriers. He was no longer simply a "Polish Pope," but a pope who was adopted and loved by men and women of every culture. Even non-Catholics were drawn to him, resulting in *Time Magazine* naming him "Man of the Year" in 1994.

His popularity and mass appeal also caught the attention of those who despised the Catholic Church and the Gospel of Jesus Christ. Throughout his papacy, John Paul II was the focus of several assassination attempts. Some of the attempts stemmed from the plotting of Islamic extremists linked with Osama bin Laden, while the most famous attempt on his life by Mehmet Ali Ağca in Saint Peter's Square was ultimately linked back to the KGB in Russia.[62] There was even an assassination attempt that came from a mentally ill priest in Spain who thought John Paul II was a Communist.[63] John Paul II was at the top of many different people's lists.

At the same time, even though he had a high profile in the world, John Paul II still remembered his friends in central Wisconsin and maintained personal contact with them. For example, Mary Jane Zdroik continued to exchange letters with the Polish Pontiff over the years and when her husband Maynard died in 1997, John Paul II sent her a personalized condolence card.[64] He still remembered his visit to Portage County, but more importantly he remembered the people he met there.

A Saint Before His Death

At the start of the new Millennium, while John Paul II ushered the world into a new era, his own time on earth appeared to be limited. His health declined rapidly and it was clear that he would not be Pope much longer. Rumors began to develop that he would soon step down as Supreme Pontiff and retire, thus abdicating his papacy. These rumors were well founded, for John Paul II later confessed that he considered the possibility of letting someone else with more youth and vigor lead the Catholic Church. He had traveled the world, but now it was becoming much more difficult and he eventually became confined to his apartment in the Vatican. In the end, however, he felt called to continue serving the Church until his Father in Heaven called him home. He saw that it was in fact his suffering that best served mankind and he would not do anything to trade the gift he had been given.[65]

His beautiful example of suffering leadership during his final years confirmed for many what they had already known; John Paul II was a living saint. This prompted many people to erect commemorations in his honor, realizing his enormous legacy and preparing for his eventual canonization. In central Wisconsin this desire to honor the pope who walked in their midst was displayed visibly by a bronze statue commissioned by Saint Peter's Catholic Church in Stevens Point. In 1997, Saint Peter's parish was celebrating the one hundred year anniversary of the dedication of their current church building and so it was fitting to celebrate the visit of Cardinal Karol Wojtyła and to make a permanent memorial of the historic event. The bronze statue entitled the "Joyful Mother Memorial" featured Pope John Paul II kneeling in prayer before the Blessed Virgin Mary holding the child Jesus in her arms and was shipped in from Italy.[66] It was then blessed and dedicated by Bishop Raymond L. Burke of the Diocese of La Crosse with the assistance of Archbishop Zenon Grocholewski, who was the Secretary of the Apostolic Signatura.[67] In addition to being a memorial of John Paul II's visit to Saint Peter's Church, the impressive statue was specifically commissioned by the pastor, Father Gerald Fisher, to commemorate the pope's encyclical *Evangelium Vitae* on building a "culture of life."[68] Father Fisher commented on the statue that, "Joyful mothers are the world's best hope for building a culture of life" and he also added that "he hoped this artwork would inspire many to say a 'Hail Mary' as they pass by for the intention of strengthening the pro-life cause."[69] Bishop Burke was so impressed by the statue that he declared, "I'm not a prophet, but I suspect this new work of art is going to draw people from near and far who will be much inspired by it."[70] The monument showed to all how deeply loved John Paul II was and how he truly inspired many by his own witness of holiness.

A Day of Mourning

Then came the fateful day of April 2, 2005. After serving the Catholic Church as Supreme Pontiff for over twenty-six years, Pope John Paul II fell victim to his increasingly bad health and died at 9:37 PM in his Vatican apartment. He died on the eve of one of his most beloved feasts, the Solemnity of Divine Mercy Sunday, a feast he instituted in the year 2000 after the inspiration of Saint Faustina Kowalska. It was a tragic day. Thousands of pilgrims mourned his death in Saint Peter's square. The Mass of Christian Burial was held on April 8 and turned out to be one of the largest funerals in recorded history. At least 300,000 people from around the world filled Saint Peter's square, with many more thousands of pilgrims extending down the Via della Conciliazione all the way to the Tiber River.[71]

When the Poles in central Wisconsin heard about his death, many sought ways to mourn. The statue of John Paul II that was erected outside of Saint Peter's church in Stevens Point became a focal point for those grieving the loss of such a beloved friend. Dozens of flowers were placed in front of the bronze statue and many more came simply to offer a prayer of thanksgiving for the blessing he was in their life. Even young people who never met John Paul II in person participated in this visible act of mourning. Most realized that they would never make it to Rome for the funeral or to pray at his place of final rest, so the statue allowed them to make an act of love to a friend who was no longer with them on earth. He was dearly loved and missed in central Wisconsin, but it did not take long for those tears to turn to rejoicing.

"Santo Subito!"

Upon the death of John Paul II, newly elected Pope Benedict XVI dispensed with the usual five-year waiting period to begin the cause for canonization. John Paul II was widely held as a living saint during his life and Pope Benedict decided to begin the lengthy process immediately. For most of those at his funeral Mass, five years seemed like an eternity and they expressed their desire by holding up signs that read in Italian "Santo Subito!;" which is roughly translated into English as "Sainthood Now!" It is not surprising that the process, which usually takes several decades to complete, was completed in only nine years.

The cause for canonization was officially opened on June 28, 2005, and after examining his entire life Pope Benedict confirmed the declaration of John Paul II's "heroic virtues" on December 19, 2009.[72] He could now be called "Venerable Servant of God" and the faithful were encouraged to actively beseech his intercession for a miracle. This was an important first step, since the next phase of the process depended heavily upon the tangible evidence of a miraculous event that was made possible through the heavenly intercession of John Paul II.

Throughout the next several years, professionals would examine many purported miracles and go through a series of tests to verify their authenticity. The first miracle that was verified, which paved the way for his beatification, was the healing of a religious sister in France. Sister Marie Pierre Simon, a member of the Congregation of Little Sisters of Catholic Maternity, was miraculously healed of Parkinson's disease through the intercession of John Paul II, which was the same ailment that had led to his own death.[73] Pope Benedict confirmed the authenticity of the miracle on January 14,

2011, and proclaimed that he would be known as "Blessed" at a ceremony in Rome on May 1, 2011.[74]

After the beatification, the cause for canonization required one additional miracle to solidify his sainthood. The final miracle that paved the way for John Paul II to be named a "Saint" occurred on the same day of his beatification and resulted in the healing of a Costa Rican woman from a brain aneurysm.[75] Pope Francis confirmed this miracle on July 5, 2013 and set the date for his official canonization to be on Divine Mercy Sunday, April 27, 2014.[76] The event was entirely unique as John Paul II was canonized alongside one of his predecessors, Pope John XXIII. Pope Francis saw that they had a lot in common and were pillars of the Second Vatican Council. It was one of the most unique events in Catholic Church history and quickly became known as the day of "Four Popes" on account of the presence of both Pope Francis and Pope Emeritus Benedict XVI at the canonization of two of their predecessors. The world came out again to celebrate the life of John Paul II, with over 800,000 people in attendance with millions more watching the ceremony via live broadcast around the world.[77] John Paul II was now officially recognized as a "Saint" in the Catholic Church, yet the canonization only confirmed a truth that many people already knew. Those who met him, either when he was a pope, a cardinal, a priest or an aspiring actor, all had the same experience of being in the presence of a saint.

Epilogue

A Saint has Walked Among Us

When reading the lives of saints, it is easy to be inspired by their fantastic stories and to be in awe at the extraordinary works they accomplished while on this earth. At the same time, we sometimes fail to realize they were human just like us. The saints may have accomplished many heroic deeds, but they too were inspired by the numerous holy men and women who went before them, and only desired to follow in their footsteps. In every age there are men and women, priests and religious, married and single, who look to Christ and see the sacrifices He made for them and are thereby strengthened to live a holy life. These men and women consequently lead lives of holiness that are beautiful and attractive and are beacons of hope for others. The saints provide concrete examples for us and call "each Christian to be a pilgrim on the pathway of beauty, truth, good, in journeying to the Celestial Jerusalem where we will contemplate the beauty of God in a relation full of love, face-to-face."[78] It is my hope that, after reading this short book, you will be inspired by the beautiful life of a simple Polish cardinal and try to walk in his footsteps.

Simplicity. Humility. Holiness.

More concretely, during his tour of rural Portage County Cardinal Karol Wojtyła showcased three virtues that everyone noticed, which stood out as beacons of light. Father Chester Zielinski, pastor of Saint Peter's Church at the time, recounted that Cardinal Wojtyła's "most distinctive characteristics [were] 'his simplicity; his humility; absolutely his humility. It is something that draws you to him.'"[79] Bishop Freking, bishop of the Diocese of La Crosse at the time, also saw these two primary attributes of the future Pope and added a third, saying, "He is first a holy man, a simple and humble man with a pleasant smile."[80] This simplicity and humility displayed itself while eating breakfast with the Sisters of Saint Joseph in Stevens Point. Sister Carlene Blavat, SSJ-TOSF, remembers an impressive man who cleaned his plate when he was done. She recounts how he "wiped up every last bit of egg and bacon with his bread. His plate looked like it had been washed!"[81]

Everyone was attracted to this man who truly practiced what he preached. He was not a cleric "too good" to get his hands dirty—he did not take his position in the Catholic Church as a free pass to have everyone wait on him. No, he was a man of Christ who took the lowest seat, served others, and found joy in the ordinary things of life.

Love of Children

Not only was he a holy, simple and humble man, but fittingly he possessed a great love of children. A reporter for the *Milwaukee Journal*, John Anderson, wrote that his love for children "was so obvious. He always reached out for them wherever they were during his visit here."[82] Even the reporters for the *Stevens Point Journal* noticed, "He shook more hands, carried children in his arms and made frequent jokes. Few people seemed nervous in his presence and he spoke as if to old friends."[83] No one knew at the time that he would be elected Pope two years later and become one of the biggest "celebrities" in the Catholic Church. For most of the people of central Wisconsin, it really did not matter—they knew holiness when they saw it and were already inspired by the example that he set. He was with them for little over 24 hours, yet permanently transformed numerous lives. Saints have a tendency to do that.

An Example For Us All

In the end, everyone who met Cardinal Karol Wojtyła during his trip to central Wisconsin was captivated and inspired by his example of servant leadership. After that day, many people hoped that he would become the next Pope. In fact, during the year of two conclaves in 1978, many who had met him in 1976 began to pray for his election to the papacy. They recognized his holiness and wanted the Vicar of Christ to be a witness of Christ.

His simple example of holiness, from his tour of farms in the countryside to the brief, yet profound visit to the nursing homes of Stevens Point, still speaks to us today. Cardinal Wojtyła, in his words and actions, shows to us that saints are not only meant to be great bastions of holiness in a secluded monastery; they can climb silos as well.

As a result of Saint John Paul II's witness, we can see that sanctity is not something only to be practiced within the four walls of a convent or rectory, but is in fact supposed to be shared with the world. This is certainly an understanding we badly need in our modern world. With fewer members of religious orders and a sparse number of priests (even though both numbers are now on the rise), we need lay people "in the world" to be beacons of light pointing to Christ.

And how do we attain this type of sanctity that puts us on the "narrow road" of perfection? Well, if we start with the example of a Polish cardinal, we can strive to be more humble, simple and holy in the ordinary experiences of our lives. We can look at his footsteps and try to follow them like a child tries to walk in the shadow of his father. If we truly want to attain perfection, we can strive to be like children and so be named "greatest in the kingdom of Heaven."

Acknowledgments

I would like to thank many people who have made this book a reality. First of all, I would like to thank my wife for supporting me and giving me encouragement when I needed it. Secondly, I would like to thank the staff at the Archives of the University of Wisconsin-Stevens Point, for their assistance in researching this book. In particular, I would like to thank Leon Ostrowski, Gayle Zivney and the Polish Heritage Awareness Society of Central Wisconsin for their support of the project and for connecting me with the people and families who still remember Karol Wojtyła's visit as if it were yesterday.

Additionally, I would like to thank the many people who contributed to this project to keep it going, especially Father Samuel Martin and Father Alan Guanella. Also, I would like to thank John Minarcin, Franz Klein and Kathryn Husing for offering their assistance in shaping the book and offering constructive criticism that was extremely helpful.

Lastly, I would like to thank Bishop William Patrick Callahan for his gracious support and assistance with this project and for allowing me access to the Archives of the Diocese of La Crosse. In the end, I owe a debt of gratitude to many people who helped with this book and am most thankful to God for inspiring me to put this most treasured memory into print.

Bibliography

Boniecki, Adam. *The Making Of The Pope Of The Millennium: Kalendarium of the Life of Karol Wojtyła.* Stockbridge: Congregation of Marians of the Immaculate Conception, 2000.

Evert, Jason. *Saint John Paul the Great: His Five Loves.* Lakewood: Totus Tuus Press, 2014.

Goc, Michael J. *Native Realm: The Polish-American Community of Portage County, 1857–1992.* Friendship: New Past Press Inc., 2001.

Pontifical Council for Culture. The Via Pulchritudinis: Privileged Pathway for Evangelisation and Dialogue. (2006). http://www.vatican.va/roman_curia/pontifical_councils/cultr/documents/rc_pc_cultr_doc_20060327_plenary-assembly_final-document_en.html

Stanbary, Jeremy D. *The Dramatic Vision of Karol Wojtyla: A "Theater of the Word," A Concise and Revealing Analysis of Pope John Paul II's Inspirational Vision for the Theater and the Arts,* 2003.

Svidercoschi, Gian Franco. *Stories of Karol: The Unknown Life of John Paul II.* Liguori: Liguori Publications, 2007.

Talley, James, et. al., ed. *Jesus, the Living Bread: A Chronicle of the Forty-First International Eucharistic Congress, Philadelphia, Pennsylvania, August 1976.* Plainfield: Logos International, 1976.

Weigel, George. *Witness to Hope: The Biography of Pope John Paul II.* New York: HarperCollins, 2001.

Notes

1   Soroka, Waclaw. "How it Happened that Cardinal Karol Wojtyla, Metropolitan of Krakow, was Invited and Accepted the Invitation to come to Stevens Point."

2   Weigel, George. Witness to Hope: The Biography of Pope John Paul II. New York: HarperCollins, 2001, 28.

3   Ibid.

4   Ibid.

5   Ibid.

6   Ibid, 29.

7   Ibid, 32.

8   Ibid.

9   Ibid, 31.

10 Ibid.

11 Stanbary, Jeremy D. The Dramatic Vision of Karol Wojtyla: A "Theater of the Word," A Concise and Revealing Analysis of Pope John Paul II's Inspirational Vision for the Theater and the Arts, 2003, 8.

12 Svidercoschi, Gian Franco. Stories of Karol: The Unknown Life of John Paul II Liguori: Liguori Publications, 2007, 59.

13 Ibid, 123.

14 Weigel, 89.

15 Ibid, 190.

16 Author's interview with Stan Potocki on April 25, 2014.

17 Goc, Michael J. Native Realm: The Polish American Community of Portage County, 1857–1992. Friendship: New Past Press Inc.: 2001, 22.

18 Ibid, 31.

19 Ibid.

20 Ibid, 50.

21 Ibid, 88.

22 Ibid.

23 Ibid, 134

24 Ibid, 136.

25 Ibid.

26 Ibid, 137.

27 Obituary of Zofia "Olenka" Aleksandra Soroka, Boston Funeral Home, May 22, 2011, Accessed on March 17, 2014,

http://bostonfuneralhome.net/?action=1&value=12&obituaries_action=2&obituaryid=120422&obituaries_page=9

28 Goc, 138.

29 Goc, 86.

30 Ibid, 139.

31 Ibid.

32 Whelan, Patrick. "Diocesan laity excited over pope." The Times Review, October 19, 1978, 3.

33 Ibid.

34 Zdroik, Mary Jane. "Mary Jane Zdroik on 1976 visit of future Pope John Paul II." Interview by Pat Snyder, WSAU 99.9 FM, May 5, 2011.

35 Smith, Peter. "Pittsburgh-area Catholics remember two popes fondly." Pittsburgh Post-Gazette, April 20, 2014, Accessed April 24, 2014, http://www.post-gazette.com/local/region/2014/04/20/Pittsburgh-area-Catholics-remember-two-popes-fondly/stories/201404200109.

36 Author's interview with Dr. Arthur Herman, April 25, 2014

37 Anderson, John. Letter addressed to Waclaw Soroka, August 19, 1983.

38 Ibid; Kimbrough, Conrad. "The Ex-Episcopalians." Sursum Corda! (Spring 1996), Accessed May 27, 2014, http://www.ewtn.com/library/ANSWERS/EX-EPIS.HTM.

39 Strybel, Robert. "Katyn priest Monsignor Peszkowski dies at 89, Polish Art Center." Polish Art Center, Accessed on August 12, 2014, http://www.polartcenter.com/Articles.asp?ID=177 .

40 Ibid.

41 Banquet Program for the "Annual Lectures on Poland," August 23, 1976.

42 "He will never be forgotten here," Stevens Point Journal, August 24, 1976, 17.

43 John Paul II, Ecclesia de Eucharistia (2003), §24, http://www.vatican.va/holy_father/special_features/encyclicals/documents/hf_jp-ii_enc_20030417_ecclesia_eucharistia_en.html.

44 Wojtyła, Cardinal Karol. "The Eucharist and Man's Hunger for Freedom." L'Osservatore Romano, October 26, 1978, 8, Accessed on November 25, 2013, http://www.ewtn.com/library/Doctrine/EUCHCONG.HTM.

45 "He will never be forgotten here."

46 Ibid.

47 Boniecki, Adam. The Making Of The Pope Of The Millennium: Kalendarium of the Life of Karol Wojtyła. Stockbridge: Congregation of Marians of the Immaculate Conception, 2000, 234.

48 "He will never be forgotten here."

49 Power, Laura. "Beatified Pope's Stay In Pomfret Recalled." Vermont Standard, June 15, 2011, http://www.thevermontstandard.com/2011/06/beatified-pope%E2%80%99s-stay-in-pomfret-recalled/,

50 Weigel, 237.

51   Ibid.

52   Ibid, 245.

53   Zdroik Interview.

54   Mary Jane Zdroik Interview by Pat Synder.

55   Author's Interview with James Cooper, August 18, 2014.

56   John Paul II, Corpus Christi Homily, Castelgandolfo, June 5, 1980, translation from the Italian by Father Samuel Martin.

57   Ibid.

58   Ibid.

59   Interview with James Cooper.

60   Diocese of La Crosse. "His Work." *Father Walijewski Guild,* Accessed on February 19, 2015, http://www.frjoesguild.org.

61   Schifrin, Nick. "Vatican Clears Former Popes John Paul II, John XXIII for Sainthood." ABC News, July 5, 2013, Accessed on August 6, 2014, http://abcnews.go.com/International/vatican-clears-popes-john-paul-ii-john-xxiii/story?id=19589227.

62   Evert, Jason. Saint John Paul the Great: His Five Loves. Lakewood: Totus Tuus Press, 2014, 158, 155.

63   Ibid, 155.

64   Zdroik Interview.

65   Evert, 200.

66   Slattery, Patrick. "Statue blessing crowning touch." *The Times Review,* September 25, 1997, 4.

67   From inscription on the base of statue.

68   Slattery, 4.

69   Ibid.

70   Ibid, 1.

71   "Pope John Paul II Buried in Vatican Crypt-Millions around the World Watch Funeral." CNN, April 9, 2005, Accessed on August 5, 2014, http://web.archive.org/web/20080613162604/http://www.cnn.com/2005/WORLD/europe/04/08/pope.funeral/index.html.

72   "Timeline of the Cause for Pope John Paul II." EWTN, Accessed on August 29, 2014, http://www.ewtn.com/johnpaul2/cause/timeline.asp.

73   Fox, Zoe. "It's Beatification Time! Pope Benedict XVI Confirms Pope John Paul II's First Miracle." TIME, January 14, 2011, Accessed on August 29, 2014, http://newsfeed.time.com/2011/01/14/its-beatification-time-pope-benedict-xvi-confirms-pope-john-paul-iis-first-miracle/.

74   "Timeline of the Cause for Pope John Paul II"

75   "Costa Rican woman speaks of John Paul II miracle." Catholic Herald, July 9, 2013, Accessed on August 29, 2014, http://www.catholicherald.co.uk/news/2013/07/09/costa-rican-woman-speaks-of-john-paul-ii-miracle/.

76   Richert, Scott P. "The Coming Canonization of Pope John Paul II." About.com, July 9, 2013, Accessed on August 29, 2014, http://catholicism.about.com/b/2013/07/09/the-coming-canonization-of-pope-john-paul-ii.htm.

[77] Smith-Spark, Laura, et. Al. "Sainthood for John Paul II and John XXIII, as crowds pack St. Peter's Square." CNN, April 28, 2014, Accessed on September 1, 2014, http://edition.cnn.com/2014/04/27/world/pope-canonization/index.html.

[78] Pontifical Council for Culture. The Via Pulchritudinis: Privileged Pathway for Evangelization and Dialogue. (2006). §II.2 http://www.vatican.va/roman_curia/pontifical_councils/cultr/documents/rc_pc_cultr_doc_20060327_plenary-assembly_final-document_en.html

[79] Enwright, Thomas. "Priest sees friend become pope." The Times Review, October 19, 1978, 3.

[80] Medinger, Daniel. "Bishop calls Polish pope an ideal choice." The Times Review, October 19, 1978, 3.

[81] O'Brien, Joseph and Stan Gould. "Diocesesan priests reflect on a pair of pope-saints." The Catholic Times, May 1, 2014, 9.

[82] Anderson.

[83] "He will never be forgotten here."

Printed in the United States
By Bookmasters